Apposition in contemporary English is the first full-length treatment of apposition. Derived from the Survey of English Usage Corpus of Written British English, the Brown University Standard Corpus of Present-day American English, and the London-Lund Corpus of Spoken British English, it provides detailed discussion of the linguistic characteristics of apposition and of its usage in various kinds of speech and writing. These include press reportage, fiction, learned writing and spontaneous conversation. Charles Meyer demonstrates the inadequacies of previous studies and argues that apposition is a grammatical relation (like complementation and modification) realized by constructions having particular syntactic, semantic and pragmatic characteristics, of which certain are dominant. Thus, syntactically, apposition is most frequently a relation between two juxtaposed noun phrases having a syntactic function (such as a direct object) promoting end-weight. Semantically, it is typically a relation between two referentially related units, the second of which adds specificity to the interpretation of the first. Pragmatically, different kinds of apposition have different communicative functions.

STUDIES IN ENGLISH LANGUAGE

Executive Editor: Sidney Greenbaum
Advisory Editors: John Algeo, Rodney Huddleston, Magnus Ljung

Apposition in contemporary English

Studies in English Language

The aim of this series is to provide a framework for original studies of present-day English. All are based securely on empirical research, and represent theoretical and descriptive contributions to our knowledge of national varieties of English, both written and spoken. The series will cover a broad range of topics in English grammar, vocabulary, discourse and pragmatics, and is aimed at an international readership.

Already published

Christian Mair   *Infinitival complement clauses in English*

Forthcoming

Jan Firbas   *Functional sentence perspective in written and spoken communication*
John Algeo   *A study of British-American grammatical differences*

Apposition in contemporary English

CHARLES F. MEYER

Department of English, University of Massachusetts at Boston

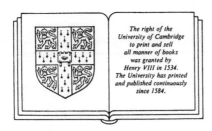

The right of the
University of Cambridge
to print and sell
all manner of books
was granted by
Henry VIII in 1534.
The University has printed
and published continuously
since 1584.

CAMBRIDGE UNIVERSITY PRESS

Cambridge

New York   Port Chester   Melbourne   Sydney

CAMBRIDGE UNIVERSITY PRESS
Cambridge, New York, Melbourne, Madrid, Cape Town, Singapore, São Paulo

Cambridge University Press
The Edinburgh Building, Cambridge CB2 2RU, UK

Published in the United States of America by Cambridge University Press, New York

www.cambridge.org
Information on this title: www.cambridge.org/9780521394758

First published 1992
This digitally printed first paperback version 2006

A catalogue record for this publication is available from the British Library

Library of Congress Cataloguing in Publication data
Meyer, Charles F.
Apposition in contemporary English / Charles F. Meyer.
        p.   cm.–(Studies in English language)
     Includes bibliographical references and index.
     ISBN 0 521 39475 9 (hardcover)
     1. English language–Apposition.   I. Title.   II. Series.
PE1395.M49   1992
425–dc20   91-18533 CIP

ISBN-13 978-0-521-39475-8 hardback
ISBN-10 0-521-39475-9 hardback

ISBN-13 978-0-521-03313-8 paperback
ISBN-10 0-521-03313-6 paperback

To my parents: Charles and Mary Meyer

Contents

5.1 The predominance of certain syntactic and semantic
     characteristics of apposition   123
5.2 Dialect and genre variation in the use of appositions   125
5.3 Apposition as a gradable relation   130
5.4 The relative frequency of apposition in relation to other
     grammatical relations   133
5.5 Future research   134

     Appendix 1   Grammatical tags   135
     Appendix 2   Appositions in individual samples of the corpora 139

     Notes   143
     References   148
     Index   151

Figures

Preface

Apposition is a grammatical category discussed in most scholarly grammars, from Jespersen's *A modern English grammar on historical principles* to Quirk *et al.*'s *A comprehensive grammar of the English language*. But despite the fact that apposition has been widely discussed, it remains a category that is poorly understood. An investigation of Jespersen, Quirk *et al.*, or any of the other sources that discuss apposition reveals numerous disagreements about how apposition should be defined and a wide variety of different kinds of constructions that are considered appositions. In this book, I attempt to clarify the confusion surrounding the category of apposition by both defining apposition and detailing its usage in computer corpora of spoken and written British and American English.

In Chapter 1, I demonstrate the inadequacies of previous treatments of apposition and argue that apposition is a grammatical relation (like complementation and modification) realized by constructions having particular syntactic, semantic, and pragmatic characteristics. In subsequent chapters, I describe these linguistic characteristics of apposition in detail, using three computer corpora of English as the basis of my study: the Survey of English Usage Corpus of Written British English, the Brown University Standard Corpus of Present-day American English, and the London–Lund Corpus of Spoken British English. In Chapter 2, I detail the syntactic characteristics of apposition, covering such topics as the various forms and functions that units in apposition have and the relationship between apposition and grammatical relations such as modification and complementation. In Chapter 3, I discuss the semantic characteristics of apposition, outlining the semantic relations between units in apposition, the semantic classes into which appositions can be classified, and the kinds of appositions that can be restrictive and nonrestrictive. In Chapter 4, I detail the pragmatic characteristics of apposition, discussing both the thematic structure of appositions and the communicative reasons why some kinds of appositions occur only in certain genres. In the final chapter (Chapter 5), I discuss apposition within the context of the grammar of English. I demonstrate that while units in apposition can have a variety of different syntactic and semantic characteristics, some of these characteristics are

xiv   **Preface**

more common that others. In addition, variation in the use of appositions is motivated not by dialectal differences between British and American English but by the varying functional needs of the various genres in which appositions occur.

I owe a deep debt of gratitude to a number of individuals and institutions who made the writing of this book possible. I am very grateful to Sidney Greenbaum, whose extensive comments on a draft of this book improved it immeasurably. Without Sidney's keen insights into the English language and expert editorial skills this book would not have been possible. I also wish to thank the Joseph P. Healey Foundation of the University of Massachusetts, which funded the initial research; Sue Horton and Neal Bruss of the English Department at the University of Massachusetts at Boston, who as, respectively, chair and associate chair provided both moral and institutional support that greatly eased my writing; and David Chin of the Computing Centre of the University of Massachusetts at Boston, whose computational skills made possible the statistical analyses presented in this book. Final thanks go to Stephanie Meyer, whose love and support over the years have been invaluable.

1   Apposition as a grammatical relation

In surveying past treatments of apposition, I demonstrate in this chapter that they provide either an inadequate or incomplete definition of apposition, and argue that apposition is best defined as a grammatical relation realized by constructions having specific syntactic, semantic, and pragmatic characteristics (1.1). To study these linguistic characteristics of apposition, I analyzed the appositions in three computer corpora of spoken and written English (1.2) with the aid of a problem-oriented tagging program (1.3).

1.1   The inadequacy of past studies of apposition

A survey of the literature on apposition supports Quirk *et al.*'s (1985:1302) assertion that "Grammarians vary in the freedom with which they apply the term 'apposition'..."

Some sources take a very conservative approach to defining apposition. Both Fries (1952:187) and Francis (1958:301) restrict the category of apposition to coreferential noun phrases that are juxtaposed:[1]

> (1) *The President of the United States, George Bush*, spoke at a campaign breakfast yesterday.

Others have expanded the category of apposition considerably. Curme (1931) admits as appositions a diverse group of constructions, including predicate appositives (p. 30):

> (2) He came home *sick*. [italics in original][2]

appositive genitives (p. 84):

> (3) the vice *of intemperance*

apposition proper (pp. 88–91), which can be loose (example 4) or close (example 5), categorizations that correspond in this study to, respectively, nonrestrictive and restrictive apposition (see 3.3):

> (4) Mary, *the belle* of the village

> (5) my friend *Jones*

and appositive adjectives (p. 93):

> (6) the room *above*

Jespersen (1961), like Curme, quite liberally defines apposition. Among the constructions he considers appositional are certain kinds of clauses in apposition with noun phrases (vol. III, p. 27):

> (7) their idea (notion, impression, view, sentiment, doctrine, etc.) that priests are infallible.

certain kinds of reflexive pronouns in apposition with the pronouns that trigger them (vol. VII, p. 172):

> (8) *You yourself* must set some tasks.

and certain kinds of participles that stand in apposition with the subject of the sentence (vol. V, p. 406):

> (9) *He* sat *smoking*.

Instead of simply listing constructions in apposition, other sources take a more principled approach. Burton-Roberts (1975:410) admits as appositions only those constructions that can be linked by a marker of apposition, constructions ranging from noun phrases (such as the apposition in example 1) to sentences (example 10) and adverbials (example 11):

> (10) You won't be totally alone, that's to say, there'll be others to help you.

> (11) They met *here*, [that's to say] *in London*.

Matthews (1981:223) claims that apposition is an "undifferentiated" grammatical relation, specifically a type of "juxtaposition," a grammatical relation that stands in opposition to other grammatical relations: modification, complementation, parataxis, coordination, and peripheral elements. Because apposition is an undifferentiated relation, Matthews (1981:224) observes, it is often difficult to distinguish apposition from other relations, and he provides numerous examples (pp. 224–36) of constructions on gradients between apposition and other relations, such as modification and parataxis.

Quirk *et al.* (1985:1302) note various characteristics of units in apposition:

(i)   Each of the appositives can be separately omitted without affecting acceptability of the sentence.
(ii) Each fulfils the same syntactic function in the resultant sentences.
(iii) It can be assumed that there is no difference between the original sentence and either of the resultant sentences in extralinguistic reference.

Appositions satisfying all criteria are termed instances of FULL APPOSITION (Quirk *et al.* 1985:1302):

(12a) *A neighbour, Fred Brick,* is on the telephone.
(12b) *A neighbour* is on the telephone.
(12c) *Fred Brick* is on the telephone. [italics in original]

Appositions not fulfilling all criteria are termed instances of PARTIAL APPOSITION (Quirk *et al.* 1985:1303):

(13a) *An unusual* present was given to him for his birthday, *a book on ethics.*
(13b) *An unusual present* was given to him for his birthday.
(13c) *Was given to him for his birthday, *a book on ethics.*

In addition to noting syntactic characteristics of apposition, Quirk *et al.* (1985:1308–16) classify appositions into various semantic classes. For instance, appositions in which the second unit provides an example of the first unit are placed into a semantic class called "exemplification" (pp. 1315–16):

(14) They visited *several cities,* for example *Rome and Athens.*

Other types of appositions are classified into other semantic classes, such as appellation, identification, and particularization.

Although all of the above approaches to defining apposition provide insights into the category of apposition, taken individually, they provide either an inadequate or an incomplete description of apposition. If, as Fries (1952) and Francis (1958) advocate, only coreferential noun phrases are considered appositions, then the class of apposition is severely limited, and a key similarity between certain kinds of nominal and non-nominal appositions is obscured: the ability of both kinds of appositions to admit a marker of apposition. In example 15, the marker of apposition *i.e.* separates two adjectives; in example 16, the marker *that is* separates two subordinate clauses.

(15) The woman was *happy* (i.e. *ecstatic*) that she was appointed chief executive of the company.

(16) *If students study hard,* that is, *if they do all of their homework and attend their classes regularly,* they will graduate from college with the credentials necessary to obtain a good job.

To claim, then, that the constructions in examples 15 and 16 are not appositions simply because they are not noun phrases is arbitrary and also ignores the obvious linguistic similarity between nominal and non-nominal appositions that contain identical markers of apposition.

Admitting a wide variety of constructions as appositions, on the other hand, expands the class of apposition to the point that virtually any construction satisfying the literal definition of apposition (i.e. "placed alongside of") is considered appositional. For instance, there is little evidence that constructions in Curme's (1931:93) category of appositive adjectives (e.g. *the room above*) behave like other appositions: such constructions do not admit a marker of apposition (e.g. **the room, that is, above*) and they are not related by any of the semantic relations, such as coreferentiality, that exist between units in apposition.[3] Consequently, considering such constructions appositional makes the category of apposition meaningless.

Although positing principles to account for appositions avoids the problem of Curme's and Jespersen's approaches to apposition, the principle posited by Burton-Roberts (1975) is problematic in certain instances. If appositions are restricted to only those units that are able to be separated by a marker of apposition, then constructions such as the one in example 17a will not be admitted as appositions, since they do not allow a marker of apposition (example 17b):

> (17a) *Mrs. Thatcher, one of the more important political figures in England since World War II,* may again run for Prime Minister.
> (17b) *Mrs. Thatcher, that is to say, one of the more important political figures in England since World War II, may again run for Prime Minister.

While Burton-Roberts considers such constructions reduced relative clauses, they behave more like appositions (Meyer 1987a:106–8). Like many other appositions, the units in constructions such as 17a can be reversed (example 18), and a copular relationship exists between them (example 19):

> (18) One of the more important political figures in England since World War II, Mrs. Thatcher, may again run for Prime Minister.
>
> (19) Mrs. Thatcher is one of the more important political figures in England since World War II.

More importantly, however, if such constructions are not juxtaposed (example 20a), a relative clause paraphrase is not possible (example 20b). The ungrammaticality of sentence 20b suggests that the second unit in this sentence is not a reduced relative but rather the second unit of an apposition.

> (20a) *The man is difficult to work with, an unsurly individual who scowls at just about everyone he encounters.*
> (20b) *The man is difficult to work with, who is an unsurly individual who scowls at just about everyone he encounters.

While Matthews (1981) notes important differences between apposition and relations such as complementation and coordination, strictly speaking, apposition is not a type of juxtaposition, since it is possible for many units in apposition not to be juxtaposed:

(21) *Three people* attended the meeting: *Dr. Smith, Professor Jones, and Mr. King*.

In addition, because apposition is a grammatical category that is realized by so many different kinds of constructions, it makes more sense to say that apposition is a relation itself rather than an instance of another type of relation, juxtaposition. Further evidence for this analysis is the fact that Matthews' relation of juxtaposition is a rather ad hoc relation, consisting of categories, such as apposition and correlative constructions (e.g. *the more, the merrier*), that do not fit easily into the other relations that Matthews posits.

Quirk *et al.* (1985) provide a conceptually sound analysis of some important syntactic and semantic characteristics of apposition. However, their analysis is incomplete because it does not provide a comprehensive discussion of the syntactic, semantic, and pragmatic characteristics of units in apposition. And it is providing this kind of comprehensive linguistic description of apposition that is the goal of this study. Apposition, it will be demonstrated, is best viewed as a grammatical relation that stands in opposition to relations such as complementation or modification. The relation of apposition is realized by constructions having specific syntactic, semantic, and pragmatic characteristics that both define the relation of apposition and distinguish it from other grammatical relations. Figure 1.1. lists the grammatical relations to which apposition is opposed and the linguistic characteristics that define the relation of apposition.[4]

According to the view of apposition depicted in Figure 1.1, the highlighted units in example 22 qualify as an apposition because they possess specific syntactic, semantic, and pragmatic characteristics.

(22) *The president of the company, Mary Smith*, resigned yesterday.

Syntactically, the units exhibit characteristics of apposition because they are noun phrases, a syntactic form that typical appositions have (2.1.1), and because they are functioning as subject of the sentence, a common syntactic function for short appositions (2.2). In addition, the units have a linear (2.3) and hierarchical (2.4) structure characteristic of many appositions: the units are juxtaposed and constitute a single apposition consisting of units that stand in a binary relation to one another.

Semantically, the units exhibit characteristics of apposition as well: the units are coreferential, one type of semantic relation that exists between units in apposition (3.1.1.1); they are in the semantic class of appellation, a class in which the second unit names the first unit (3.2.1.2); and they are

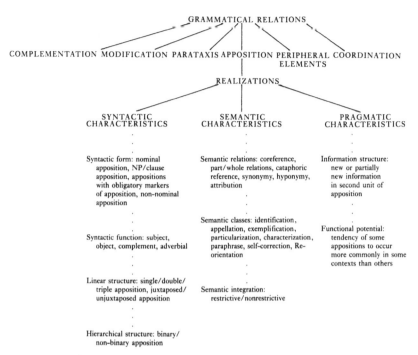

Fig. 1.1 The linguistic characteristics of units in apposition

nonrestrictive and therefore not semantically integrated, because the second unit does not restrict the reference of the first unit (3.3).

Pragmatically, the units exhibit characteristics of apposition because the second unit contains new information not previously introduced into the discourse (4.1). And because the second unit contains new information that names the first unit, the apposition has a functional potential best suited to the press genre, a genre in which it is communicatively necessary to name individuals and provide information about them (4.4.2.3).

The linguistic characteristics of the apposition in example 22 represent some of the many characteristics that appositions can have. A complete description of these characteristics is given in Chapters 2–4, which discuss, respectively, the syntactic, semantic, and pragmatic characteristics of units in apposition. In addition, Section 2.5 discusses constructions whose linguistic characteristics place them on gradients between apposition and other relations, such as complementation.

Defining apposition in the manner proposed in this study avoids the inadequacies of past treatments of apposition. Viewing apposition as a grammatical relation having various realizations does not arbitrarily restrict the class of apposition to only certain kinds of constructions. At the same time, the class of apposition is expanded in a principled manner so that only

Fig. 1.2 Corpora

A Brown Corpus (60 samples: 120,000 words)
   1 Press (20:40,000)
   2 Learned (20:40,000)
      (a) Humanistic (10:20,000)
      (b) Scientific (10:20,000)
   3 Fiction (20:40,000)

B London-Lund Corpus (LLC) (24 samples: 120,000 words)
   1 Spontaneous conversation (24:120,000)
      (a) Disparates (8:40,000)
      (b) Equals (8:40,000)
      (c) Intimates/equals (8:40,000)
      (d) Intimates (8:40,000)

C Survey of English Usage Corpus (SEU) (24 samples: 120,000 words)
   1 Press (8:40,000)
   2 Learned (8:40,000)
      (a) Humanistic (4:20,000)
      (b) Scientific (4:20,000)
   3 Fiction (8:40,000)

certain kinds of constructions are considered appositional. Finally, the linguistic characteristics posited to define apposition cover not just some characteristics of apposition but all of them.

1.2 The computer corpora used to investigate apposition

To detail the various linguistic characteristics of apposition and also to study its usage, three computer corpora of English served as the basis of this study: the London-Lund Corpus of Spoken British English (cf. Svartvik and Quirk 1980; and Svartvik 1990), the Survey of English Usage Corpus of Written British English (see Greenbaum 1985), and the Brown University Standard Corpus of Present-day American English (see Kučera and Francis 1967). Approximately 120,000 words of text in each of these three corpora was investigated, making the total corpus on which this study is based approximately 360,000 words in length. The corpora, as Figure 1.2 indicates, enabled the study of four types of variation. The Brown and Survey of English Usage corpora were used to compare British and American English. Within these corpora, equal proportions of journalistic, learned, and fictional writing were selected to study variation by written

Fig. 1.3 Sample tagging routine

Example sentence
The word capitalism can no doubt be defined in the terms of
reasonably strict economic analysis, yet it gains its colour very
largely from what people believe capitalist society has been like.
(SEU w.9.3.5-3)

Tags
(A)   Corpus: SEU (Tag 3)
(B)   Genre: learned (humanistic) (3)
(C)   Sample: w.9.3 (91)
(D)   Reference: specific (2)
(E)   Syntactic form: citation (14)
(F)   Syntactic function: subject (non-existential) (1)
(G)   Multiple apposition: single apposition (1)
(H)   Juxtaposed/unjuxtaposed apposition: juxtaposed (1)
(I)   Binary/non-binary apposition: distinction not relevant (3)
(J)   Optional markers of apposition: no marker (6)
(K)   Semantic relation: strict coreference (1)
(L)   Semantic class: identification (3)
(M)   Restrictive/nonrestrictive apposition: restrictive (1)

---

genre. The London-Lund Corpus was compared with the Brown and
Survey of English Usage corpora to study variation in speech and writing
and, additionally, variation by speech genre. To investigate this last type of
variation, the spontaneous conversation of four different kinds of individuals
was investigated: disparates, equals, intimates, and intimates and equals.
All of the frequency counts reported in this book are based on the
appositions occurring in these three corpora of written and spoken British
and American English.

1.3 The computational analysis of appositions in the corpora

To study appositions in the corpora, a problem-oriented tagging routine
was developed.[5] Each apposition was identified and manually assigned
thirteen different tags. The tags recorded such information as the corpus,
genre, and sample in which the apposition occurred. In addition, the tags
specified linguistic information about the apposition, for instance the
syntactic form and function of the apposition, the semantic relationship
existing between the units, and so forth. A complete listing of tags is given
in Appendix 1. A sample tagging routine for an example apposition is
detailed in Figure 1.3.

Lotus 1–2–3[TM], a popular spreadsheet, was used to computerize the tags assigned to each apposition and to create a tag-file. This file was downloaded onto a DEC VAX/VMS mainframe computer and analyzed statistically with a program entitled SPSS, "The statistical package of the social sciences" (see Nie *et al.* 1975).[6] This program was used to provide frequency information about appositions in the corpora, for instance the number of appositions in each of the three corpora, the number of appositions in each genre, the number of restrictive versus nonrestrictive appositions, and so forth.[7]

2   The syntax of apposition

Apposition is a grammatical relation having various syntactic characteristics, characteristics which will serve as the focus of this chapter.

The relation of apposition is realized by a variety of syntactic forms (2.1): noun phrases predominantly (2.1.1) but other syntactic forms as well (2.1.2–2.1.4). Although these forms can have a full range of syntactic functions, they most commonly have two: subject and object (2.2). In addition, the forms making up the two units of an apposition have a linear (2.3) and hierarchical (2.4) structure that differentiates the relation of apposition from other relations, such as modification and complementation. However, like other grammatical relations, apposition is a gradable relation (2.5): some appositions are fully appositional; other appositions behave in a manner that places them on a gradient between apposition and other grammatical relations, such as coordination (2.5.2), peripheral elements (2.5.3), modification (2.5.4), and complementation (2.5.5).

2.1 The syntactic form of units in apposition

The three corpora contained a total of 2,841 constructions counted as appositions in this study (Table 2.1).[1] Approximately three-quarters of these appositions were evenly distributed among the written samples of British and American English. A much smaller percentage (27 percent) occurred in the spoken samples. This distribution indicates that overall there is little difference in the occurrence of appositions in written British and American English but that there is considerable variation in their use in spoken and written English. This variation has a pragmatic explanation: appositions are communicatively more important in speech than in writing (4.3).

The appositions in the corpora, as Table 2.1 shows, consisted of two units that had four general syntactic forms: two noun phrases (example 1), a noun phrase followed by a clause or sentence (example 2), two units (most frequently noun phrases) joined by an obligatory marker of apposition (example 3), or two units one or both of which was a sentence, a clause, or a phrase other than a noun phrase (example 4):

Table 2.1. *Syntactic forms of appositions in the corpora*

Form	Brown	LLC	SEU	Total
Nominal apposition	647	282	637	1,566 (55%)
NPs in apposition with clauses or sentences	152	100	164	416 (15%)
Appositions with obligatory markers of apposition:				
NP + NP	81	137	107	325 (11%)
Other	19	14	15	48 (2%)
Non-nominal apposition	127	245	114	486 (17%)
Total	1,026 (36%)	778 (27%)	1,037 (37%)	2,841 (100%)

(1) *The first twenty thousand pounds, the original grant,* is committed. (LLC s.1.2 782–3)[2]

(2) There is perhaps no value statement on which people would more universally agree than *the statement that intense pain is bad.* (Brown J52 220–30)

(3) It is one of the main purposes of this chapter to show how the effects gained by the use of metaphor are related to its linguistic form, and this purpose will be furthered if it can be shown that consideration of its linguistic form makes it easier to deal with *problems* such as *those touched on in the last few paragraphs.* (SEU w.9.4.56-1)

(4) [Thomas] More stands on the margins of modernity *for one reason alone – because he wrote Utopia.* (Brown J57 450–60)

Even though apposition is a relation realized by a variety of syntactic forms, it is predominantly a relation between two noun phrases: as Table 2.1 illustrates, 1,891 (or 67 percent) of the appositions in the corpora contained units consisting either of two noun phrases or of noun phrases separated by an obligatory marker of apposition.

2.1.1 *Nominal apposition*

Table 2.2 lists the number of appositions in the corpora consisting of units that were various kinds of noun phrases. As the table demonstrates, proper nouns figured prominently in nominal appositions: slightly fewer than half of the nominal appositions in the corpus consisted of appositions in which

Table 2.2. *Types of NPs in nominal appositions*

Form	Brown	LLC	SEU	Total
Proper NP (one or both units)	360	45	256	661 (42%)
Common NP (both units)	171	142	149	462 (30%)
Misc. NPs	94	28	202	324 (21%)
Pronouns (one or both units)	22	67	30	119 (7%)
Total	647 (41%)	282 (18%)	637 (41%)	1,566 (100%)

Table 2.3. *Appositions centred around proper nouns*

Form	Brown	LLC	SEU	Total
NP (d) + proper NP	83	7	77	167
NP (−det) + proper NP	97	1	31	129
Proper NP + NP (−det)	65	0	56	121
Proper NP + NP (d)	38	13	43	94
Proper NP + NP (i/a)	42	4	35	81
NP (i) + Proper NP	29	9	13	51
Other	6	11	1	18
Total	360	45	256	661

−det = NP lacking determiner
d = definite
i = indefinite
i/a = indefinite/attributive

one or both units were a proper noun; the other types of nominal appositions occurred much less frequently.

2.1.1.1 *Proper nouns*

Proper nouns occurred in appositions having six primary syntactic forms (Table 2.3). Two of the more frequent of these forms consisted of a proper noun in apposition with a unit lacking a determiner. In example 5, the first noun phrase in the apposition lacks a determiner; in example 6, the second noun phrase does.

> (5) Britain's plans to press Russia for a definite cease-fire timetable was announced in London by *Foreign Secretary Lord Home.* (Brown A21 138–400)

> (6) About 45,000 people would lose their homes as a result of the Greater London Council's 1,000 million road plans,

Mr. Douglas Jay, Labour MP for Battersea North and former President of the Board of Trade, said last night. (SEU W.12.4.61–2)

The appositions in examples 5 and 6, as Table 2.3 demonstrates, occurred predominantly in the written corpora, particularly in the Brown Corpus; within the written corpora, their occurrence was restricted primarily to journalistic writing, a distribution motivated by communicative factors (4.4.2.3).[3]

While a number of sources have discussed the syntactic structure of appositions whose first units lack determiners (cf. Bell 1988 and Rydén 1975), little has been said about the relationship between this type of apposition and the type containing a second unit without a determiner. If the structure of both types of appositions is compared, the close interrelationship between the two appositions can be seen.

Table 2.4. *Underlying determiners in units of appositions lacking a determiner*

Determiner	Brown	LLC	SEU	Total
Article (F)	96	0	30	126
Article (S)	65	0	56	121
Possessive pro (F)	1	1	1	3
Possessive pro (S)	0	0	0	0
Total	162	1	87	250

F = Appositions containing an initial unit without a determiner
S = Appositions containing a second unit without a determiner

Table 2.4 details the type of determiner implied in units lacking a determiner. Bell (1988:336) notes that in appositions containing an initial unit lacking a determiner the underlying determiner is more commonly an article (example 7) than a possessive pronoun (example 8). Table 2.4 demonstrates that the same holds true in appositions whose second units lack a determiner (example 9).

(7) *[The] State Party Chairman James W. Dorsey* added that enthusiasm was picking up for a state rally to be held Sept. 8 in Savannah at which *[the] newly elected Texas Sen. John Tower* will be the featured speaker. (Brown A01 900–20)

(8) Mrs Renora Gilliburn, *[her] daughters Tracey and Diane*, and Mr Gilliburn escaped unhurt. (SEU W.12.70.3)

(9) Miss Mercouri was supported by *Stathis Pangoulis, [the] brother of the condemned man*. (SEU W.12.3e–4)

Table 2.5 lists the various kinds of modification existing in units lacking determiners. As this table demonstrates, the type of modification present in

Table 2.5. *Types of modification in units of appositions lacking a determiner*

Form	Brown	LLC	SEU	Total
No modification				
First unit	45	0	14	59
Second unit	4	0	1	5
One premodifier				
First unit	33	1	11	45
Second unit	12	0	1	13
Multiple premodifiers				
First unit	17	0	6	23
Second unit	12	0	3	15
Postmodifier(s)				
First unit	2	0	0	2
Second unit	24	0	34	58
Pre- and postmodifier(s)				
First unit	0	0	0	0
Second unit	13	0	17	30
Total	162	1	87	250

the unit depends crucially on whether the unit is first in the apposition or second. If the unit is first, it is more likely, as both Bell (1988:336) and Rydén (1975:20) observe, to contain either no premodification (example 10) or one premodifier (example 11) than multiple premodification (example 12) or any postmodification (example 13).

> (10) *Pitcher* Steve Barber joined the club one week ago after completing his hitch under the Army's accelerated wintertime military course, also at Fort Knox, Ky. (Brown A11 1140–60)

> (11) Sellers was able to talk, even joke, today with his bride of two months – *Swedish star* Britt Ekland, who has been by his bedside almost constantly during the crisis hours. (SEU W.12.2.17)

> (12) ENGLAND *international left-winger* Eddie Holliday will never touch "bubbly" again. (SEU W.12.2.52)

> (13) *Secretary of Labor* Arthur Goldberg will speak Sunday night at the Masonic Temple at a $25-a-plate dinner honoring Sen. Wayne L. Morse, D-Ore. (Brown A10 940-50)

On the other hand, if the unit lacking a determiner occurs in the second unit, no modification is rare (example 14) and postmodification quite common (example 15).

> (14) The committee for the annual Central City fashion show has been announced by Mrs. D.W. Moore, *chairman*. (Brown A17 380–90)

Table 2.6. *Structure of proper NP occurring with units of appositions lacking determiners*

Structure of NP	Brown	LLC	SEU	Total
Full name				
First unit	86	0	23	109
Second unit	48	0	3	151
Surname				
First unit	8	0	4	12
Second unit	1	0	0	1
First name				
First unit	0	0	0	0
Second unit	3	1	1	5
Honorific/title				
First unit	0	0	3	3
Second unit	16	0	53	69
Total	162	1	87	250

(15) LORD BLAKENHAM, *chairman of the party*, said that he sensed growing confidence and determination in Conservative ranks. (SEU W.12.1–24, 1–25)

In addition, modification by both a predmodifier and postmodifier is quite frequent (example 16).

(16) Mr. Sidney Miller, 63, *elected member of the Legislative Council for West Falkland*, is extremely suspicious of the British Government's intentions. (SEU W.12.4.32)

The patterns of complexity illustrated in Table 2.5 demonstrate the close relationship between apposition and premodification: because appositions containing a first unit lacking a determiner are on a gradient between apposition and premodification (2.5.4.1), such units are not likely to be complex, since extensive premodification in English often leads to stylistically awkward constructions (Quirk *et al.* 1985:1342). On the other hand, if the unit lacking a determiner occurs in the second unit of the apposition, complexity is less of a problem.

Table 2.6 details the structure of the proper noun occurring with units lacking a determiner. If the proper noun occurs in the second unit of the apposition, it is more likely to be a complete name (example 17) than only a surname (example 18), since the occurrence of only a surname "implies full titleness" in the first unit (Bell 1988:336).

(17) A citation from Conservation Commissioner *Salvatore A. Bontempo* credits his supervision with a reduction in the number of forest fires in the state. (Brown A06 1180–200)

(18) She [Mrs. Blanche Dunkel] had been sentenced to 180 years in prison, but former Gov. *Stratton* commuted her term to 75 years, making her eligible for parole, as one of his last acts in office. (Brown A20 1660–80)

Table 2.6 also demonstrates that the occurrence of only a first name in the second unit is rare (example 19), despite the fact that Bell (1988:336) claims that the informality of such constructions makes the use of only a first name highly likely.

(19) Charley Simonelli, top Universal-International film studio exec, makes an honest man out of this column. As we bulletin'd way back, he'll wed pretty Rosemary Strafaci, of the Golf Mag staff, in N.Y.C. today. Handsome bachelor *Charley* was a favorite date of many of Hollywood's glamor gals for years. (Brown A16 1280)

While full names were the norm if the proper noun occurred in the second unit of the apposition, they were not common if the proper noun occurred first in the apposition. In this case, the structure of the proper noun was determined by whether it occurred in a sample of British or American English. Such constructions in American English favored the full first name (example 20).

(20) MARSHALL FORMBY of Plainview, former chairman of the Texas Highway Commission, suggested a plan to fill by appointment future vacancies in the Legislature and Congress, eliminating the need for costly special elections. (Brown A02 930–60)

In British English, in contrast, they more commonly contained an honorific or title (example 21).

(21) The trade unions are fighting the redundancies, and *Mr. John Allen*, district secretary of the Engineering Union, said the strike would continue until management "entered into constructive negotiations with the trades unions." (SEU w.12.7i.3)

The more frequent occurrence of an honorific or title in British English reflects perhaps a greater concern for formality in the British press than the American press (4.4.2.3).

The remaining appositions in this category, as Table 2.3 illustrates, consisted of various combinations of proper nouns and common nouns. Most common were proper nouns in apposition with definite noun phrases (example 22 and 23).[4]

(22) *This chap Robbe Grillet* starts from nothing at all, and although the overwhelming impression at the end of the book is

Table 2.7. *Appositions containing common nouns*

Form	Brown	LLC	SEU	Total
NP (i) + NP (i)	63	69	57	189
NP (d) + NP (d)	50	47	41	138
NP (i) + NP (d)	18	13	27	58
NP (d) + NP (i)	15	7	13	35
NP (d) + NP (i/a)	19	5	11	35
Other	6	1	0	7
Totals	171	142	149	462

d = definite
i = indefinite
i/a = indefinite/attributive

> that we know what it felt like to be jealous, but it wasn't worth the effort of finding out. (LLC s.3.1 321–9)

> (23) The Orioles got a run in the first inning when *Breeding, along with Robinson, the two Birds who got a pair of hits*, doubled to right center, moved to third on Russ Snyder's single to right and crossed on Kunkel's wild pitch into the dirt in front of the plate. (Brown A11 500–30)

Less common were proper nouns in apposition with two kinds of indefinite noun phrases: those containing an attributive indefinite article (example 24) or a specific indefinite article (example 25).[5]

> (24) The new school superintendent is *Harry Davis, a veteran agriculture teacher*, who defeated *Felix Bush, a school principal and chairman of the Miller County Democratic Executive Committee*. (Brown A10 1700–20)

> (25) Could we return to *a play that you say you know pretty well, Macbeth*? (LLC s.3.5 1106–7)

2.1.1.2 *Common nouns*

The next most frequently occurring nominal appositions consisted of units that were noun phrases headed by common nouns (Table 2.7). Occurring most frequently were units that were both indefinite noun phrases (example 26) or definite noun phrases (example 27).

> (26) What I think we need, you see, is rooms with *a table, a table which students can sit round*. There's no sense in a seminar where someone is sitting at one end of the room and all the students are looking down towards the, the person who's sort of chairing it. (LLC s.3.4 47–57)

Table 2.8. *Appositions centered around miscellaneous NPs*

Form	Brown	LLC	SEU	Total
Citations	40	12	113	165 (51%)
Symbols, abbreviations, formulas, quotes, element names, titles	11	1	52	64 (20%)
Card NPs	21	12	24	57 (18%)
Percentages, measurements, dates, addresses, temperatures	22	3	13	38 (12%)
Total	94	28	202	324 (100%)

Card = Noun phrase preceded by cardinal number

> (27) With a ball-point pen he wrote it down in *the weather proforma – the oblong card which chimed the hours on the darkened flight-deck –* and passed it back so that the engineer could add the fuel available, the navigator could put in their position, and the radio officer could send it to Control. (SEU w.16.4.59–1, 59–2)

Occurring far less frequently were appositions in which the first unit was indefinite and the second definite (example 28), or in which the first unit was definite and the second indefinite (example 29) or attributive (example 30).

> (28) He [Johnnie] had *an easy masculine grace* about him, *the kind that kids don't have, but that I had sometimes admired in other older men.* (Brown P22 3209–340)

> (29) Consider *the features of Utopian communism: generous public provision for the infirm; democratic and secret elections of all officers including priests; meals taken publicly in common refectories; a common habit or uniform prescribed for all citizens; even houses changed once a decade* ...(Brown J57 1640–80)

> (30) The Association of Head Mistresses warmly welcomed *the Newsom report – "a vital and moving human document" –* but was convinced that a "crash" programme of recruitment was essential to provide teachers who were alert to new ideas and adaptable to changing times. (SEU w.12.1–46)

2.1.1.3 *Miscellaneous noun phrases*

A number of nominal appositions contained miscellaneous types of noun phrases fitting into the categories depicted in Table 2.8. Nearly half of these appositions contained one unit which was a citation form, a construction which does not always have the typical form of a noun phrase but which behaves like a noun phrase in all other respects:

(31) The words *German, Catholic* and *Jew* stand respectively for a nation, a Church and a race. [italics in original] (SEU w.9.3.6–1, 6–2)

(32) In the double sentence *The smaller the town, the friendlier the people* it [the dominant stress] will generally be on the subjects *the town* and *the people*. [italics in original] (Brown J33 24–6)

Also quite common were appositions in which one unit consisted of a common noun preceded by a cardinal number:

(33) *One such instance* [of Fromm's misuse of important terms] has already been presented: *his use of alienation.* (Brown J63 1840–50)

(34) Waterlogging leads to *three kinds of changes in the soil*: *physical, biological and chemical.* (SEU w.9.6.14)

Occurring with varying frequency almost exclusively in the written corpora (4.4.2.4) were miscellaneous appositions one or both of whose units consisted of such noun phrases as a measurement (example 35), a date (example 36), a temperature reading (example 37), an abbreviation (example 38), or a formula name (example 39).

(35) *The diameter of the antenna beam, 6.7 feet,* was small enough to allow resolution of some of the larger features of the lunar surface, and contour diagrams have been made of the lunar brightness distribution at three lunar phases. (Brown J01 1370–400)

(36) Board members indicated Monday night this would be done by an advisory poll to be taken on *Nov. 15, the same date as a $581,000 bond election for the construction of three new elementary schools.* (Brown A10 900–30)

(37) Investigation of the high-temperature form, Phase I, is more difficult, particularly because at *the temperatures of measurement,* namely *150 °C. and 200 °C.,* the severe loss of intensity at the higher angles, occasioned by the increased thermal vibrations, limits the amount and precision of the neutron diffraction data. (SEU w.9.8.180–2, 181–1)

(38) In addition one serum was obtained from *a donor (R.E.)* who had been sensitized 6 years previously. (Brown J09 026–7)

(39) With a higher soil pH *the element phosphorus* (and others) becomes more available for absorption by plant roots. (SEU w.9.6.26–27)

2.1.1.4 *Pronouns*

The least frequent type of nominal apposition contained one or (less commonly) two units that were pronouns (Table 2.9). In appositions of this type, it was most common for the first unit to be a definite pronoun and the second unit to be a definite noun phrase:

(40) Well, *it*'s a jolly nice place, *the new university*, but one, one, doesn't sort of leap up and down and say much, you know, because it's a modest sort of place. (LLC s.1.10 435–9)[6]

(41) Pointing at some television cameras, Mr. Wall said: "The cameras are not on you, they are on *them* (*the chanting students*). You are not news. You will not be news until you wake up from your apathy." (SEU w.12.4.47)

However, there did occur in the corpora infrequent occurrences of appositions whose units were a definite pronoun and a noun phrase with an attributive indefinite article (example 42), or various combinations of indefinite pronouns and indefinite noun phrases (examples 43 and 44).

(42) Moss, a man who knows how much the cannery helps the county, doesn't believe it will close. But *he* is in the middle, *an employee of DeKalb*, but on the side of the people. (Brown B08 390–420)

(43) He [Bunyans] has [applied for the position], I think, and there was *nothing to tell him that he might be excluded*, *nothing in the job as advertised*. (LLC s.2.6 17–21)

Table 2.9. *Appositions centred around pronouns*

Form	Brown	LLC	SEU	Total
Pro (d) + NP (d)	9	40	12	61
Pro (i) + NP (i)	1	5	5	11
Pro (d) + NP (i/a)	3	2	1	6
Pro (i) + pro (i)	2	1	0	3
NP (i) + pro (i)	0	2	1	3
Other	7	17	11	35
Total	22	67	30	119

d = definite
i = indefinite
i/a = indefinite/attributive

(44) Here was *one familiar face, someone who had survived.* (SEU
w.12.3f–1)

2.1.2 *Noun phrases in apposition with clauses or sentences*

While it was quite common for two noun phrases to be in apposition, it was
less common for a noun phrase to be in apposition with a subordinate clause
or a sentence (Table 2.10). As Table 2.10 illustrates, noun phrases were
much more frequently in apposition with subordinate clauses than they
were with sentences.

Table 2.10. *NPs in apposition with clauses or sentences*

Form	Brown	LLC	SEU	Total
NP + clause	98	78	133	309
NP + sent	41	19	16	76
Sent + NP	12	2	15	29
Other	1	1	0	2
Total	152	100	164	416

2.1.2.1 *Nominal/clausal apposition*

Table 2.11 provides a breakdown of the types of noun phrases and
subordinate clauses that were in apposition in the corpora. Most frequently
in apposition were noun phrases followed by *that-* and *to-*clauses. The
majority of these appositions consisted of a definite noun phrase followed
by a *that-*clause:

(45) Milman Parry rigorously defended *the observation that the
extant Homeric poems are largely formulaic,* and was led to

Table 2.11. *NPs in apposition with clauses*

Form	Brown	LLC	SEU	Total
NP (d) + *that-*clause	51	39	89	179
NP (i) + *that-*clause	14	10	13	37
NP (d) + *to-*clause	14	1	11	26
NP (i) + *to-*clause	13	2	9	24
NP (d) + other clauses	2	2	5	9
Pro (d) + clause	2	24	4	30
Other	2	0	2	4
Total	98	78	133	309

d = definite
i = indefinite

postulate that they could be shown entirely formulaic if the complete corpus of Greek epic survived. (Brown J67 017–21)

Occurring much less frequently were indefinite noun phrases followed by *that*-clauses (example 46) and definite and indefinite noun phrases followed by *to*-clauses (examples 47 and 48).

(46) He [Houston] had *a lowering feeling that he had somehow missed the bus, that some of the virtue had gone out of him in the past year.* (SEU w.16.7.26–4)

(47) The first speaker was Amos C. Barstow who had been unanimously chosen president of the meeting. He spoke of *his desire to promote the abolition of slavery by peaceable means* and he compared John Brown of Harper's Ferry to the John Brown of Rhode Island's colonial period. (Brown J58 1420–60)

(48) Sikhs meeting in London yesterday approved *a plan to try to suppress publication of future immigration speeches by Mr Enoch Powell.* (SEU w.12.3f–1)

Tables 2.12 and 2.13 list examples of noun phrases in the first units of *that*- and *to*-appositions that occurred more than five times in the corpora. In *that* appositions (Table 2.12), only one noun phrase – *fact* – occurred with any regularity:

(49) *The fact that the testimony of the Spirit takes an objective form in a people and words and actions* preserves it from the arbitrariness of subjectivism and individualism. (SEU w.9.2.144–2, 144–3)

In *to*-appositions, while no one noun phrase predominated, nearly three-

Table 2.12. *NPs heading first units of that-appositions*

NP	No. of occurrences
fact	85 (39%)
feeling	8
view	7
impression	6
suggestion	6
assumption	6
idea	5
news	5
theory	5
Other	83
Total	216

Table 2.13. *NPs heading first units of to-appositions*

NP	No. of occurrences
tendency	9
decision	7
plan(s)	6
desire	5
bid	2
failure	2
purpose	2
wish	2
Other	15
Total	50

Table 2.14. *Nominalized and non-nominalized NPs in the first units of that- and to-appositions*

Form	Nominalized	Non-nominalized	Total
That-apposition	101 (47%)	115 (53%)	216 (100%)
To-apposition	41 (82%)	9 (18%)	50 (100%)
Total	142 (53%)	124 (47%)	266 (100%)

quarters of the appositions contained the eight noun phrases listed in Table 2.13, with the noun phrase *tendency* occurring most frequently:

> (50) ...there is *a tendency to confine the word 'history' to what can be put into a serious history book*, and perhaps taught with safety and without controversial overtones in schools and colleges. (SEU w.9.3.1–1, 1–2)

Table 2.14 calculates the frequency with which the noun phrases in the first units of *that-* and *to*-appositions were nominalized or non-nominalized noun phrases. While most noun phrases in *to*-appositions were nominalized noun phrases such as *tendency* in example 50 above, far fewer noun phrases in *that*-appositions were nominalized noun phrases. However, the majority of non-nominalized noun phrases in *that*-appositions (85) were the noun phrase *fact*. If this noun phrase is not counted, far fewer (30, or 14 percent) of the noun phrases in the first units of *that*-appositions were non-nominalized noun phrases.

While *that-* and *to*-clauses were the most common kinds of clauses in apposition with noun phrases in the corpora, two other kinds of constructions also occurred (Table 2.11). Definite noun phrases occasionally

Table 2.15. *NPs in apposition with sentences*

Form	Brown	LLC	SEU	Total
Sentence + NP (i/a)	12	2	15	29
Card NP + sentence	14	4	6	24
Pro (d) + sentence	9	9	1	19
NP (d) + sentence	11	3	4	18
NP (i) + sentence	7	3	5	15
Other	1	1	0	2
Total	54	22	31	107

d = definite
i = indefinite
i/a = indefinite/attributive
Card = noun phrase preceded by cardinal number

occurred in apposition with clauses containing such subordinators as *whether*:

> (51) The phenomenon [of reliving a strong emotion] raises *the question whether the guidance of the emotions for therapeutic ends may not have an even wider application in the area of the neuroses.* (Brown J17 1570–90)

Pronouns occurred in apposition with a variety of types of clauses, such as the *-ing* participle clause in example 52 and the *to*-infinitive clause in example 53.

> (52) I did apply to Birkbeck, you know, but I found *it* so difficult, *working in the day and trying to study.* (LLC s.3.1 1065–8)

> (53) Yes, *that* would be rather uncommon, *to have no sort of food taboos and so forth.* (LLC s.1.6 581–3)

These kinds of appositions, as Table 2.11 illustrates, were particularly common in the spoken corpus.

2.1.2.2 *Nominal/sentential apposition*
As Table 2.15 indicates, no one type of noun phrase in apposition with a sentence occurred with any great frequency in the corpora. Occurring most frequently were sentences in apposition with either an attributive noun phrase (example 54) or a noun phrase containing a cardinal number (example 55).

> (54) Mercantile's growth is far more broadly based than before, a factor which has enabled the group to live with high interest

rates and still keep a firm grip on margins. (SEU w.12.6a–5, 6a–6)

(55) We might, therefore, ask *two things* about a new theory of a change of stage:
a. *Does it give a satisfying physical picture of what is probably happening?*
b. *Is the numerical agreement with the observed facts in keeping with the number of adjustable parameters, or is the theory unduly "forced" in this respect?* (SEU w.9.9.22–1, 22–2)

Occurring slightly less frequently were sentences in apposition with a pronoun (example 56), a definite noun phrase (example 57), and an indefinite noun phrase (example 58).

(56) He'll burn himself out if he goes on at this rate. Think *that*'s the general feeling really: *He does seem to overdo it.* (LLC s.1.6 687–90)

(57) *The last question in the interview* was the one I was itching to hear all the way through, namely, *Isn't it a bit of a risk to set up a risk manager's?* (LLC s.2.11 1105–10)

(58) It was then that Picasso and Braque were confronted with *a unique dilemma*: they had to choose between illustration and representation. (Brown J59 1200–10)

2.1.3 *Appositions containing obligatory markers of apposition*

Markers of apposition can be either optional or obligatory. In example 59a, the marker of apposition *that is* is optional: its omission does not lead to an ungrammatical construction (59b).

(59a) It's like a cube; that is, either it can be convex or it can be concave. (LLC s.1.8 934–6)
(59b) It's like a cube: either it can be convex or it can be concave.

In example 60a, on the other hand, the marker *particularly* is obligatory: its omission leads to an ungrammatical construction (60b).

(60a) Upon receiving the news [of the slave rebellion of 1859], Northern writers, editors, and clergymen heaped accusations of murder on the *Southern states*, particularly *Virginia*. (Brown J58 300–10)
(60b) *... heaped accusations of murder on the Southern states, Virginia.

Because markers of apposition in examples such as 59 are optional, their use

Table 2.16. *Obligatory markers of apposition*

Marker	Brown	LLC	SEU	Total
like	18	70	17	105
such as	23	7	34	64
of	35	23	35	93
or	2	39	12	53
including	14	4	10	28
especially	4	3	5	12
particularly	1	2	6	9
for instance	0	2	0	2
mostly	1	0	1	2
even	1	1	0	2
among them	1	0	0	1
chiefly	0	0	1	1
e.g.	0	0	1	1
Total	100	151	122	373

Table 2.17. *Syntactic forms of units joined by obligatory markers of apposition*

Form	Brown	LLC	SEU	Total
NP + NP	81	137	104	322
NP + clause	16	14	13	43
Other	3	0	5	8
Total	100	151	122	373

is governed by pragmatic considerations (4.2). Markers of apposition are obligatory, however, for semantic and syntactic reasons. The semantic characteristics of constructions containing obligatory markers are discussed in 3.1.1.2; the syntactic characteristics of these constructions are the focus of this section.

Table 2.16 lists the obligatory markers of apposition that occurred in the corpora (see Table 4.3 for a listing of optional markers of apposition). As the table indicates, only five markers of apposition (*such as, like, of, or,* and *including*) occurred regularly; most markers occurred fewer than ten times.

The vast majority of the markers in Table 2.16 joined noun phrases (Table 2.17), such as those in example 60a. Far fewer markers separated other kinds of units, such as a noun phrase and a clause (example 61), two prepositional phrases (example 62), or two adjectives (example 63).

> (61) She [my mother] was getting herself so excited at *the thought* of *my auntie Elsie coming and knitting and knitting and knitting and driving her mad.* (LLC s.1.12 1043–7)

(62) How dangerous the abuses of misapplied history may be
[,] the record of the last half-century *in Europe*, particularly *in
Germany*, amply testifies, and, unless the human race is
unusually lucky, no doubt the record of the next half-century,
particularly in parts of Asia and of Africa, will confirm.
(SEU w.9.3.8–1, 8–2)

(63) The sacs form by evagination from the brain and remain
connected with the *dorsal epithalamic* or *habenular* region of the
between-brain by two stalks. (SEU w.9.7.103–2)

All of the constructions in this section are similar because they contain
obligatory markers of apposition. However, in the corpora, the constructions
differed in terms of the syntactic forms they were realized by. While
constructions consisting of markers such as *like* and *particularly* had similar
forms, those containing the markers *of* and *or* had different forms.

2.1.3.1 *Obligatory inclusive markers*
A large number of obligatory markers of apposition join constructions in
which the second unit of the apposition is included within the first.[7]
Markers of this type include *such as, like, including,* and *especially* – all of the
markers in Table 2.16 except for *of* and *or*.

Two syntactic characteristics typified appositions containing two noun
phrases joined by inclusive markers of apposition. First of all, of the 227
appositions in the corpora containing an inclusive marker, the vast majority
(204, or 90 percent) contained a first unit that was indefinite (example 64);
very few (23, or 10 percent) contained a first unit that was definite (example
65).

(64) We were willing to consider analogies but don't forget that
the analogies between teaching *something relatively simple* like
late medieval poetry was very different from Anglo-Saxon. (LLC
s.3.2 886–90)

(65) Ralph Houk, successor to Casey Stengel at the Yankee
helm, plans to bring *the entire New York squad* here from St.
Petersburg, including *Joe Dimaggio*[,] and large crowds are
anticipated for both weekend games. (Brown AII 1100–20)

Secondly, most of the first units in these types of appositions (156, or 69
percent) were plural (example 66); far fewer (71, or 31 percent) were
singular (example 67).

(66) *About 40 representatives of Scottish bodies*, including *the
parents of some of the children flown to Corsica*, were addressed
by an English surgeon and doctor and by M. Naessens. (SEU
w.12.1–40)

Table 2.18. *Inclusive markers*

Form	Brown	LLC	SEU	Total
NP (i) + marker + NP (d)	30	24	25	79
NP (i) + marker + Pro (d)	4	39	6	49
NP (i) + marker + NP (i)	16	16	17	49
Other	12	11	27	50
Total	62	90	74	227

d = definite
i = indefinite

> (67) It is a simple matter, for one so disposed, to take *a work* like *The Sane Society* and shred it into odds and ends. (Brown j63 110–20)

These syntactic characteristics are significant because, as is demonstrated in 3.1.1.2, they make the marker of apposition in these kinds of constructions semantically necessary. Without the marker, semantically implausible constructions (such as 60b) result.

Table 2.18 details the forms of both noun phrases in appositions joined by inclusive markers. It was most common for this kind of apposition to contain an initial noun phrase that was indefinite and a second noun phrase that was a definite noun phrase (example 68), a definite pronoun (example 69), or an indefinite noun phrase (example 70):

> (68) You might read *a new and original piece of criticism* such as *Eliot on Hamlet* and then you might go back to the play and look at it and say does it work. (LLC s.3.5 1014–19)

> (69) In the last eight years, *all Presidential appointments*, including *those of cabinet rank*, have been denied immediate action because of a Senate rule requiring at least a 24 hour delay after they are reported to the floor. (Brown a03 1830–60)

> (70) Since the Government's rate support grant is actually being reduced in real terms from 51.9 per cent to 48.8 per cent, *ratepayers*, especially *small businesses*, will have to pay out more, not less. (SEU w.12.8h.4)

2.1.3.2 *The obligatory marker* of
While indefinite noun phrases predominated as initial units in appositions containing inclusive markers, in those containing the marker *of* definite noun phrases predominated (Table 2.19). Three kinds of constructions

Table 2.19. Of-*apposition*

Form	Brown	LLC	SEU	Total
NP (d) + *of* + NP (d)	22	10	22	54
NP (d) + *of* + subjectless *-ing* clause	10	10	10	30
NP (d) + *of* + *-ing* clause with subject	2	3	2	7
Other	1	0	1	2
Total	35	23	35	93

d = definite

followed the initial definite noun phrase in this kind of apposition: another noun phrase that was definite or indefinite (example 71), a subjectless *-ing* participle clause (example 72), or an *-ing* clause with a subject (example 73).

> (71) It should also be recognized that *the problem* of *rural tenancy* cannot be solved by administrative decrees alone. (Brown J22 105–7)

> (72) Alphonse and Jock are extremely reluctant to start new joint degrees because it would mean *this awful process* of *putting a new thing through every board*. (LLC S.3.4 997–1000)

> (73) Members [of the House of Lords] recoiled at *the thought* of *230 voting peers drawing perhaps £2,000 a year for what Mr. Hamilton calculated might be only 45 days' work a year*. (SEU W.12.4.10)

2.1.3.3 *The obligatory marker* or

In all of the appositions discussed thus far in this section, certain forms predominated. In appositions containing the marker *or*, however, no one form predominated overwhelmingly (Table 2.20). Occurring most commonly were constructions containing either two indefinite noun phrases (example 74) or one or two proper nouns (examples 75 and 76).

> (74) So far I have been concerned solely to set out *certain associated distinctions*, or *aspects of one distinction*, which have historically been made or recognized by philosophers. (SEU W.9.1.142–1)

> (75) He [Lloyd George] entertained *Colonel House* or *whoever the American...representative was*. (LLC S.2.3 564–5)

> (76) Though they [the job candidates] all seem solid enough people to me, and in, in, the second batch we have Bunyan. It is *Bunyan*, or *Bunyans*. (LLC S.2.6 533–7)

Table 2.20. Or *apposition*

Form	Brown	LLC	SEU	Total
NP (i) + *or* + NP (i)	2	17	2	21
Proper NP + *or* + NP (i)	0	10	0	10
Proper NP + *or* + proper NP	0	6	0	6
NP (d) + *or* + NP (d)	0	1	1	2
Other	0	5	9	14
Total	2	39	12	53

d = definite
i = indefinite

Occurring relatively infrequently were constructions containing two definite noun phrases:

> (77) Cecily, *his new wife* or *his second wife*, she teaches. (LLC s.1.13 638–40)

2.1.4 *Non-nominal apposition*

Most of the appositions discussed in the previous sections contained at least one unit that was a noun phrase.[8] In this section, the focus is on non-nominal apposition. Non-nominal apposition includes constructions in which neither of the units is a noun phrase or nominal clause or constructions in which one unit is a noun phrase and the other an adjective phrase. Although non-nominal apposition of sentences was quite common (Table 2.21), non-nominal apposition of phrases, clauses, and different form classes was relatively uncommon.

2.1.4.1 *Non-nominal apposition of phrases*
Table 2.22 lists the kinds of non-nominal phrases in apposition in the corpora. Two phrases occurred most frequently: prepositional phrases (example 78) and adjective phrases, which were either attributive (79a) or predicative (79b).

> (78) The definitions in effect require us to divide the sentence into two parts which together make up the whole of it; and they *allow* us to make the division *in the way we want to make it*, i.e., *between 'Socrates' and 'is wise.'* (SEU w.9.1.145–2, 145–3)

> (79a) This circumstance in the patient's case plus the fact that his tactual capacity remained basically in sound working order constitutes its exceptional value for the problem at hand since the evidence presented by the authors is overwhelming that,

Table 2.21. *Non-nominal apposition*

Form	Brown	LLC	SEU	Total
Phrasal	39	59	41	139
Clausal	19	19	23	61
Sentential	59	159	41	259
Different form	10	8	9	27
Total	127	245	114	486

Table 2.22. *Non-nominal apposition of phrases*

Form	Brown	LLC	SEU	Total
Prep phrase	8	20	18	46
Adj phrase	17	19	9	45
Pred phrase	7	16	11	34
Verb phrase	5	2	1	8
Adv phrase	2	2	2	6
Total	39	59	41	139

> when the patient closed his eyes, he had absolutely no *spatial* (that is, *third-dimensional*) awareness whatsoever. (Brown J52 100–50)
>
> (79b) Walter's painted the whole of our extension bedroom, which is *enormous, much bigger than this room.* (LLC s.1.8 366–7)

Occurring less frequently than prepositional and adjective phrases were predicative phrases, phrases which consisted either of the entire predicate of a clause (example 80) or the entire predicate minus the operator (example 81):[9]

> (80) It [Gertrude's telling Hamlet that his mind is wandering] provides a good excuse for, for, Hamlet's killing Polonius in, in, Claudius's eyes because he, he, can claim madness for Hamlet and *get rid of him, throw him out of the country without causing any strife or political upheaval perhaps.* (LLC s.3.5 502–8)
>
> (81) Are you getting enough teaching or are you *being – please don't misunderstand me when I say this –* overtaught, that is to say, *being asked to attend more lectures, more seminars, more tutorials than you can prepare for?* (LLC s.3.3 716–24)

Table 2.23. *Non nominal apposition of clauses*

Form	Brown	LLC	SEU	Total
Clause with subordinator	10	12	15	37
To-infinitive	9	3	8	20
Other	0	4	0	4
Total	19	19	23	61

The remaining phrases – adverb phrases and verb phrases – occurred only rarely:

> (82) It snowed *softly, silently.* (Brown L06 980)

> (83) People are just beginning to *rouse* themselves, *stretch*, you know. (LLC s.1.12 662–3)

2.1.4.2 *Non-nominal apposition of clauses and sentences*
Tables 2.23 and 2.24 detail the types of clauses and sentences that were in apposition in the corpora. As Table 2.23 demonstrates, the most common kinds of clauses in apposition were *to*-infinitive clauses (example 84) and clauses headed by a subordinator (examples 85, 86, and 87).

> (84) *To treat her as a person, to offer her civilised manners*, took on with her almost the quality of an insult: only young people and innocent countries could afford to play about like this. (SEU w.16.2.97–3)

> (85) She thinks *if you say the slightest thing against her* – that is, *if you argue on the other side* – if she has an argument and you say anything at all on the other side, she thinks because you aren't absolutely with her, that you're taking the other side and completely against her. (LLC s.1.12 961–75)

> (86) Hilliard was appalled, he had not dreamed that this could happen and so quickly to a man like Garrett, to a man *who was yet not ill or wounded, who had survived for so long by careful management, perhaps, and luck.* (SEU w.16.8.62–3)

> (87) If it could be shown *that judgments of good and bad were not judgments at all, that they asserted nothing true or false, but merely expressed emotions like "Hurrah" or "Fiddlesticks,"* then these wayward judgments would cease from troubling and weary heads could be at rest. (Brown J51 070–100)

Of the clauses headed by a subordinator, nearly half (18) were headed by the subordinator *that*.

Table 2.24. *Non-nominal apposition of sentences*

Form	Brown	LLC	SEU	Total
Declarative	57	139	41	237
Interrogative	2	19	0	21
Exclamatory	0	1	0	1
Total	59	159	41	259

Because declarative sentences are the most common type of sentence in English, they were overwhelmingly, as Table 2.24 illustrates, the most common types of sentences in apposition in the corpora:

> (88) I was going to make a very stupid remark. [That is to say] I was going to say that nothing that tastes nice is poisonous. (LLC s.2.10 1444–5)

> (89) It could be seen that both artists [Brumidi and Costaggini] used a very thick final coat of plaster, one half inch, and that both followed the traditional Italian fresco technique as described by Cennino Cennini in the 14th Century, and current in Italy to this day. That is, they used opaque color throughout, getting solid highlights with active lime white. (Brown J61 690–730)

Sentences in apposition were particularly common in the spoken corpus, because in speech they serve a specific communicative function: to clarify the meaning of the first unit of the apposition (4.4.2.2).

Interrogative sentences in apposition were much less common (example 90):

> (90) What kind of category of novel would you say generally speaking *Lord of the Flies* belongs to? [That is to say] Is it a realistic novel or is it a symbolic novel or how would you describe it? (LLC s.3.1 406–12)

And while there were no examples of exclamatory sentences in apposition in the corpora, one example of subordinate exclamative clauses in apposition did occur:

> (91) And I'm astounded *how naive they* [*academics*] *are*, really, *how easily taken in.* (LLC s.1.6 353–6)

2.1.4.3 *Non-nominal apposition of different form classes*
A small number of appositions in the corpora consisted of units of completely different form classes (Table 2.25). In constructions of this type, there exists apposition by function, not by form. That is to say, unlike most

Table 2.25. *Non-nominal apposition of different form classes*

Function/form	Brown	LLC	SEU	Total
Subject complement				
Adjective + NP	3	3	1	7
NP + adjective	1	1	1	3
Other	0	0	1	1
Adverbial				
Adverb + prep ph	3	1	4	8
Other	3	2	2	7
Other	0	1	0	1
Total	10	8	9	27

of the appositions in the previous sections, which consisted of appositions having similar forms and functions,[10] the appositions in this section have different forms but identical functions: subject complement or adverbial. In examples 92 and 93, the appositions consist of adjective phrases and noun phrases functioning as subject complements:

> (92) That was *an extremely abstruse talk* in a way, *very highflown.* (LLC s.1.6 1003–6)

> (93) If the occupation of the territory by the colonial power was *wholly indefensible, the wicked work of evil men*, then perhaps everything that springs from it must be eliminated. (SEU w.9.3.5–1, 5–2)

In examples 94 and 95, the appositions consist of prepositional phrases, an adverb, and a clause, all functioning as adverbials:

> (94) He [Hilliard] knew that Garrett had a wife and four daughters *somewhere, in Worthing or Horsham or Lewes.* (SEU w.16.8.60)

> (95) More stands on the margins of modernity *for one reason alone – because he wrote Utopia.* (Brown J57 450–60)

2.2 The syntactic function of units in apposition

Table 2.26 lists the syntactic function of appositions in the corpora for which a syntactic function could be determined for at least one of the units in apposition.[11] Table 2.26 lists functions of appositions within sentences, clauses, or phrases.

Because apposition is a relation in which at least one of the units is usually a noun phrase (see 2.1.1–2.1.3), it is not surprising that nearly 88

Table 2.26. *The syntactic functions of units in apposition*

Form	Brown	LLC	SEU	Total
Subject	331	141	327	799 (33%)
Non-existential	312	120	308	740
Existential	19	21	19	59
Object	499	298	515	1,312 (55%)
Direct	155	155	171	481
Indirect	0	1	1	2
Prepositional	344	142	343	829
Complement	67	73	63	203 (8%)
Subject	64	71	61	196
Object	3	2	2	7
Adverbial	20	32	38	90 (4%)
Verb	1	2	0	3
Total	918	546	943	2,407 (100%)

percent of the appositions in the corpora had functions associated with noun phrases: subject (example 96), direct object (example 97), and object of preposition (example 98).

> (96) On the shores north and south, *the fishers and mooncursers – smugglers* – lived along the churning Great South Bay and the narrow barrier of sand, Fire Island. (Brown K16 80–3)

> (97) These are few and seemingly disjointed data, but they illustrate *the important fact that fundamental alterations in conditioned reactions occur in a variety of states in which the hypothalamic balance has been altered by physiological experimentation, pharmacological action, or clinical processes.* (Brown J17 1420–60)

> (98) Vital secrets of *Britain's first atomic submarine, the Dreadnought,* and, by implication, of the entire United States Navy's still-building nuclear sub fleet, were stolen by a London-based Soviet spy ring, secret service agents testified today. (Brown A20 010–40)

In addition to having functions associated with noun phrases, appositions had functions associated with positions in the sentence, clause, or phrase that promoted the principle of end-weight (Quirk *et al.* 1985:1361–2). As Aarts (1971) and de Haan (1987) have noted, the lengthier and more complex a noun phrase is the less likely it is to occur in the subject position of a clause. Because appositions typically consist of two noun phrases (see 2.1.1 and 2.1.3) or a noun phrase and a nominal clause (2.1.2), appositions are relatively heavy constructions. Consequently, 65 percent of the appositions in the corpora had functions associated with positions that promote end-weight: direct object (example 97), object of preposition (example 98), subject complement (example 99), and subject of sentences containing existential *there* (example 100).

> (99) I'm sure that Jack is, is, in some ways *a better man to work with, an easier man to work with* than Dan Ross. (LLC s.1.2 245–9)

> (100) There is *a marked tendency for religions, once firmly established, to resist change, not only in their own doctrines and policies and practices, but also in secular affairs having religious relevance.* (Brown J23 1790–810)

Despite the fact that the two units of an apposition create a relatively heavy construction, 31 percent of the appositions in the corpora occurred in a position that does not promote end-weight: the pre-verbal subject position (as in example 96). However, a large number of appositions in subject positions (359, or 49 percent) occurred in the journalistic style, a style containing a high number of relatively short and non-complex appositions centered around proper nouns (2.1.1):

> (101) *Comic Gary Morton* signed to play the Living Room here Dec. 18, because that's the only time *his heart, Lucille Ball,* can come along. (Brown A16 1140–60)

Since these appositions are much shorter and less complex than the appositions in examples such as 97, 99, and 100, it is not surprising that the journalistic styles of the corpora had so many appositions occurring in subject positions.

Four functions occurred relatively rarely in the corpora. The functions of adverbial (example 102) and verb (example 103) were rare, largely because the forms which typically realize these functions – verbs, adverbs, and prepositional phrases – were not forms that frequently occurred in appositions (2.1.4).

> (102) AT LEAST six Camden secondary schools and most local primary schools were closed *yesterday (Wednesday)* as a result of a one-day national strike by the National Union of Teachers in support of a pay claim. (SEU w.12.7.7d.1–2)

> (103) The *Evening News* was *finished, consumed.* (SEU w.16.4.53–2)

The function of indirect object (example 104) was rare because the position in which indirect objects occur (before direct objects) is not a position which promotes end-weight.[12]

(104) You know there was this business at the outbreak of the
First World War when the Kaiser suddenly horrified everyone
and gave *Moltke the Younger* a nervous breakdown from which
he never really recovered. (LLC s.2.3 407–12)

And the function of object complement (example 105) was rare, probably
because this is not a frequently occurring clause function.

(105) Of course there was no doubt that the child would now
have a good Christian background, but there were institutions
provided for that sort of thing, and it really was too ostentatious
of Julia to go round buying up babies and calling them *fancy
names* like *Tarquin*. (SEU w.16.3.197–1, 197–2)

2.3 The linear structure of apposition

Most appositions in the corpora were single appositions (Table 2.27); that
is, appositions in which an initial unit was in apposition with a single second
unit:

(106) It may be well to start by comparing the work of the
historian with the work of *two other groups engaged in expert
enquiries, the lawyers and the natural scientists*, and then to
discuss the historian's relationship to his own task. (SEU
w.9.3.11–4)

However, there did occur infrequent instances of double or triple
apposition. Example 107 illustrates double apposition: an initial unit in
apposition with two units that are also in apposition.

(107) This is *the bulk of the book* therefore, *chapters three and
four, sections three and four*. (LLC s.3.2 1003–6)

Example 108 illustrates triple apposition: an initial unit in apposition with
two subsequent appositions.

(108) Similarly, the innovations of bop, and of [Charlie] Parker
particularly, have been vastly overrated *by people unfamiliar with
music*, especially *by that ignoramus, the intellectual jitterbug, the
jazz aficionado*. (Brown j66 0063–6)

Both double and (in particular) triple apposition were uncommon in the
corpora; the vast majority of appositions (as Table 2.27 demonstrates) were
single appositions.

Most appositions in the corpora (Table 2.28) contained units that were
juxtaposed (example 109) rather than unjuxtaposed (example 110):

(109) She was absolutely *obstinate, self-willed*, and, and,
determined to do her thing. (LLC s.1.12 948–50)

Table 2.27. *Instances of single, double, and triple apposition*

Form	Brown	LLC	SEU	Total
Single apposition	965	686	975	2,626
Double apposition	26	40	28	94
Triple apposition	3	4	2	9

Table 2.28. *Juxtaposed and unjuxtaposed appositions*

Form	Brown	LLC	SEU	Total
Juxtaposed	950 (93%)	598 (77%)	973 (94%)	2,521 (89%)
Unjuxtaposed	76 (7%)	180 (23%)	64 (6%)	320 (11%)
Total	1,026 (100%)	778 (100%)	1,037 (100%)	2,841 (100%)

Table 2.29. *Reasons for not juxtaposing units of appositions*

Reasons	Brown	LLC	SEU	Total
End-focus/weight	32 (42%)	7 (4%)	27 (42%)	66 (21%)
Syntactic constraints	35 (46%)	64 (36%)	30 (47%)	129 (40%)
Pronoun stress	9 (12%)	52 (29%)	6 (9%)	67 (21%)
Pragmatic expressions	0	57 (32%)	1 (2%)	58 (18%)
Total	76 (100%)	180 (100%)	64 (100%)	320 (100%)

(110) *Cavendish* stood there, *a maypole round which the others executed a three-step.* (SEU w.16.4.55–2)

There were various reasons why units in apposition were not juxtaposed (Table 2.29). In the written corpora, two reasons predominated. First, a number of units were unjuxtaposed for reasons of end-focus and end-weight. In examples 111 and 112, the units of each apposition are not juxtaposed to avoid an unbalanced sentence and to focus the second unit of the apposition by placing it in the emphatic end-position of the sentence.

(111) *The following possibilities* exist for achieving this [improving the efficiency of plasma generators]: 1. *The use of high voltages and low currents by proper design to reduce electron heat transfer to the anode for a given power output.* 2. *Continuous motion of the arc contact area at the anode by flow or magnetic forces.* 3. *Feed back of the energy transferred to the anode by*

applying gas transpiration through the anode. (Brown J02 480–540)

(112) What is the use of propounding this definition? *Its use* is that of any valid definition: *to enable us to agree what comes into our discussion and what does not.* (SEU w.9.4.56–2)

Second, units of appositions were unjuxtaposed because of syntactic constraints on the placement of words in a sentence or clause. In example 113, the units are not juxtaposed because it is most natural in this context to place the adverbial *however* between the two units.

(113) They [the dishes] looked *so formidable,* however, *so demanding,* that I found myself staring at them in dismay and starting to woolgather again, this time about Francesca and her husband. (Brown R02 350–80)

In example 114, the units are not juxtaposed because syntactically the clause *aged 30* must follow the head noun phrase it modifies, a position occurring between the two units of the apposition.

(114) The Pope yesterday appealed to the Greek Government to show mercy toward *Alexandros Panagoulis,* aged 30, *the Greek army private sentenced to death in Athens for plotting to overthrow the regime.* (SEU w.12.3e–1)

In the spoken corpus, two additional reasons for not juxtaposing the units of appositions predominated. First, units were not juxtaposed because of the spontaneous, unplanned nature of speech and additionally to avoid placing too much stress on a pronoun beginning a sentence:

(115) *She*'s a shocker you know, *Lizzie.* (LLC s.1.13 699–70)

(116) *That* would be one of the most difficult things, *buckling down to Anglo-Saxon.* (LLC s.3.1 143–6)

Second, units were not juxtaposed to make room for the placement of "pragmatic expressions" (Erman 1986), parenthetic expressions such as *you know* or *I mean*:

(117) *The political reasons involved,* I mean *the ones of national prestige,* are entirely ones of timing. (LLC s.2.8 49–51)

(118) It [the beer] tasted *so watery,* you know *lifeless.* (LLC s.1.7 239–40)

2.4 The hierarchical structure of apposition

Hierarchically, apposition is typically a binary relationship: the second unit of the apposition is in apposition with the unit that immediately precedes it:

Table 2.30. *Binary and non-binary apposition*

Type	Brown	LLC	SEU	Total
Binary	43	65	42	150
Non-binary	18	27	20	65
Total	61	92	62	215

> (119) *Signor Luciano Lama, secretary-general of Italy's Communist Trade Union Federation*, told a mass meeting in Rome that the resignation of Signor Leone's government would not be the end of the struggle. (SEU w.12.4.14)

In instances of double and triple apposition, however, the relationship between the units in apposition can be either binary or non-binary. In example 120, the apposition is binary: the third unit is in apposition with the second unit; both these units, in turn, are in apposition with the first unit.

> (120) The interview had taken place on 18 November; and the news had come *one week later to the day: 25 November 1949, a Friday*. (SEU w.16.7.38–1)

In example 121, in contrast, the apposition is non-binary: the third unit is not in apposition with the second unit; instead, both units are in apposition with the first unit.

> (121) But in Goodrich's return there was really too much room for conjecture, too wide a margin of uncertainty. After all, *a figure had to be arrived at, a definite sum in pounds, shillings, and pence, a last chord in which all the conflicts and problems of the return would be resolved*. (SEU w.16.5.16–3)

As Table 2.30 shows, it was most common for apposition of this type to be binary as opposed to non-binary.

2.5 The syntactic gradient of apposition

Because apposition is primarily a relation between noun phrases, syntactic discussions of apposition have largely been concerned with the constituent structure of nominal appositions. These discussions have been marked by much disagreement and inconsistency. Haugen (1953:170), for instance, claims that appositions such as *the poet Burns* consist of a head (*Burns*) and a modifier (*the poet*). Hockett (1955:101), on the other hand, maintains that such appositions are double-headed (i.e. endocentric). Norwood (1954:268, note) avoids the issue altogether, deciding to call the initial unit of an apposition the "first noun" rather than the "head noun" because "it [head noun] suggests a structure of modification."

These varying analyses of apposition are largely the result of trying to posit one constituent structure for all types of appositions, and of failing to consider that apposition is "an undifferentiated relation" (Matthews 1981:224), a relation that cannot always be easily distinguished from other relations, such as modification or complementation. If, however, apposition is considered an undifferentiated, or gradable, relation, we can distinguish those constructions that are most appositional – central appositions – from those that are (in varying degrees) less appositional – peripheral appositions. The particular constituent structure we then assign to an apposition will depend on the extent to which the units of the apposition are structurally dependent on each other. Structural dependency, according to Allerton (1979:128), can be characterized in three ways. A construction is exocentric if both of its constituents are obligatory; subordinative if only one of its constituents is obligatory; and coordinative if none of its constituents are obligatory. Appositions can be either coordinative or subordinative. Those that are coordinative will be considered central appositions. Those that are subordinative will be considered peripheral appositions and on gradients between central apposition and coordination, peripheral elements (Matthews 1981:123f), modification, and complementation.

To identify central and peripheral appositions, we can posit the criteria below. These criteria identify the extent to which two units of an apposition are structurally independent of each other (i.e. coordinative) or structurally dependent on each other (i.e. subordinative):

(1)   The first unit of the apposition can be optionally deleted.
(2)   The second unit of the apposition can be optionally deleted.
(3)   The units of the apposition can be interchanged.

2.5.1 *Central and peripheral apposition*

Central apposition is characterized by units which are syntactically independent of each other. Consequently, to be considered a central apposition, two units must satisfy criteria 1–3.

Of the forms of apposition discussed in Section 2.1, only two forms can be central appositions: certain kinds of nominal appositions (2.1.1) and certain kinds of non-nominal appositions (2.1.4). Examples 122 and 123 provide instances of central appositions. In each of these appositions, the units can be deleted (the b and c examples) and their orders can be reversed (the d examples).

> (122a) Jean Fardulli's Blue Angel is the first top local club to import *that crazy new dance, the Twist.* (Brown A16 1880–900)

(122b) Jean Fardulli's Blue Angel is the first top local club to import the Twist.

(122c) Jean Fardulli's Blue Angel is the first top local club to import that crazy new dance.

(122d) Jean Fardulli's Blue Angel is the first top local club to import the Twist, that crazy new dance.

(123a) In this puddled soil the exchange of air between atmosphere and soil is minimised, so creating an *anaerobic* (*oxygen-deficient*) environment for roots, the so-called *reduced zone*. (SEU w.9.16.16–17)

(123b) ...so creating an oxygen-deficient environment for roots...

(123c) ...so creating an anaerobic environment for roots...

(123d) ...so creating an oxygen-deficient (anaerobic) environment for roots.

Peripheral apposition is characterized by units which are (to varying degrees) structurally dependent on each other. Examples 124 and 125 contain instances of peripheral appositions, appositions which satisfy only some of the criteria for apposition. In example 124, while each of the units can be deleted (the b and c examples), they cannot be interchanged (the d example). In example 125, the second unit can be deleted (the c example), and both units can be reversed (the d example). But because the units are not juxtaposed, the first unit cannot be deleted (the b example).

(124a) Have you ever been to *it, the Biograph*? (LLC s.2.10 671–2)

(124b) Have you ever been to the Biograph?

(124c) Have you ever been to it?

(124d) *Have you ever been to the Biograph, it?

(125a) In other regions *a tissue containing more cells and less matrix* is found, *the so-called fibro-cartilage*, and this more nearly resembles fibrous connective tissue and serves to emphasize that no sharp line can be drawn between these tissues. (SEU w.9.7.85–2)

(125b) *In other regions is found, the so-called fibro-cartilage...

(125c) In other regions a tissue containing more cells and less matrix is found...

(125d) In other regions the so-called fibro-cartilage is found, a tissue containing more cells and less matrix...

Peripheral appositions are of two types. Some constructions (such as those in examples 124 and 125) are peripherally appositional simply because they do not fulfil one or more of the syntactic criteria for central apposition.

Other constructions are peripherally appositional not just because they fulfil only some of the critera for central appositions but because they are on gradients between apposition and other relations. This latter type of peripheral apposition is discussed in the following sections.

2.5.2 *Apposition and coordination*

Quirk *et al.* (1985:1301–2) remark that apposition and coordination are similar because "not only do coordinate constructions also involve the linking of units of the same rank, but the central coordinators *and* and *or* may themselves occasionally be used as explicit markers of apposition..." Because of the close relationship between apposition and coordination, we find ambiguities between apposition and coordination and, additionally, instances of coordinative apposition and simple apposition whose constituent structures are virtually identical.

Ambiguities between apposition and coordination result because it is sometimes difficult to distinguish between apposition and asyndetic coordination. In examples 126 and 127, the juxtaposed constructions are syntactically quite similar because each satisfies criteria 1–3:

> (126a) But the head of department is *a little bit idiosyncratic, an awfully nice chap.* (LLC s.1.6 218–21)
> (126b) But the head of department is an awfully nice chap.
> (126c) But the head of department is a little bit idiosyncratic.
> (126d) But the head of department is an awfully nice chap, a little bit idiosyncratic.

> (127a) The address was in the Holborn district; it sounded *shabby, dismal.* (SEU w.16.1.19–1)
> (127b) ...it sounded dismal.
> (127c) ...it sounded shabby.
> (127d) ...it sounded dismal, shabby.

Semantically, however, the units are quite different. In example 127, *shabby* and *dismal* are in apposition because they are synonymous, a semantic relationship existing in other kinds of appositions (3.1.2.1). In example 126, on the other hand, *an awfully nice chap* and *a little bit idiosyncratic* are not synonymous. Consequently, in this construction, we have asyndetic coordination rather than apposition.

In constructions containing an overt coordinator, it is difficult, as Figure 2.1 demonstrates, to make clear syntactic distinctions between coordinative apposition and simple coordination. While the units in example 128a are coreferential and hence semantically appositional (3.1.1.1), syntactically these units behave no differently than those in example 129, which are not coreferential and therefore not appositional. In both constructions, the

Fig. 2.1 The gradient of coordinative apposition to simple coordination

Sentences:	a	b	c	d
Criteria				
1	−	−	−	−
2	−	−	−	−
3	+	+	−	−

Sentences

a Take the elevator, or lift as it's called here.

b Taxpayers should write their senators or their congressman.

c The woman's my mother, or rather my stepmother.

d He's a fine worker – and a very integral part of our operation at that.

Criteria

1 The first unit of the apposition can be deleted.

2 The second unit of the apposition can be deleted.

3 The two units can be interchanged.

units cannot be deleted (the b and c examples) but they can be reversed (the d examples).

(128a) They have a thing called *First University Examination*, or *FUE*. (LLC s.3.6 134–6)

(128b) *...a thing called or FUE.

(128c) *...a thing called First University Examination, or.

(128d) ...a thing called FUE, or First University Examination.

(129a) Taxpayers should write *their senators* or *their congressmen*.

(129b) *Taxpayers should write or their congressmen.

(129c) *Taxpayers should write their senators or.

(129d) Taxpayers should write their congressmen or their senators.

It might be argued that example 129 contains an atypical instance of coordination, since not all conjuncts in coordinate constructions can be reversed (Quirk *et al.* 1985:920). However, there also exist instances of coordinative apposition in which the units cannot be reversed. In the apposition in example 130, for instance, the units, which illustrate speaker coreference (3.1.1.1), cannot be reversed without drastically changing the meaning of the construction.

(130a) I keep thinking of *my uncle Arthur*, or rather *my great uncle Arthur*. (LLC s.1.10 6–7)

(130b) I keep thinking of my great uncle Arthur, or rather my uncle Arthur.

The situation is further complicated by the construction in example 131:

(131a) Britain, after centuries of separatism, is *rightly part of Europe* – and *a very important part at that*. (SEU w.12.8e.3)

(131b) *Britain...is and a very important part at that.

(131c) *Britain...is rightly part of Europe – and.

(131d) *Britain...is a very important part at that – and rightly part of Europe.

Like the units in example 130, the units in example 131 exhibit characteristics of both apposition and coordination: the units are semantically appositional (a relationship of hyponymy exists between them [3.1.2.3]), but they satisfy none of the syntactic criteria for apposition; in addition, if the units are made subject of the sentence, the concord with the verb is singular, a further indication that the units are in apposition rather than coordinated.

(132) Rightly part of Europe – and a very important part at that – is Britain.

But despite the quasi-appositional status of the units in example 131, it might be argued that this example contains an instance not of coordinative apposition but of appended coordination, "a loose kind of coordination in which the second conjoin is appended to the clause in which the first conjoin occurs..." (Quirk *et al.* 1985:975).

As examples 128–131 illustrate, it is extremely difficult to differentiate coordinative apposition from simple coordination: while there are clear semantic differences between the two relations, syntactically the relations are quite similar.

2.5.3 *Apposition and peripheral elements*

While it is difficult to distinguish coordination from apposition, it is somewhat easier, as Figure 2.2 illustrates, to distinguish between apposition and peripheral elements. The constructions in examples 133–135 illustrate the gradient between apposition and peripheral elements. Example 133 contains an instance of central apposition, since the units in this construction satisfy each of the syntactic criteria for apposition.

(133a) *A Texas halfback who doesn't even know the team's plays, Eldon Moritz*, ranks fourth in Southwest Conference scoring after three games. (Brown A11 010–30)

Fig. 2.2 The gradient of apposition to peripheral elements

Sentences:	a	b	c
Criteria			
1	+	+	−
2	+	?	+
3	+	?	−

Sentences
a A friend of mine, Fred Jones, visited me last night.
b A habitual criminal, Ed Lynch was sentenced to life in prison.
c Helen Smith, formerly the president of the organization, is now head of its board of directors.

Criteria
1 The first unit of the apposition can be deleted.
2 The second unit of the apposition can be deleted.
3 The two units can be interchanged.

(133b) Eldon Moritz ranks fourth...
(133c) A Texas halfback...ranks fourth...
(133d) Eldon Moritz, a Texas halfback...ranks fourth...

Examples 134 and 135 contain constructions more closely related to peripheral elements than to apposition. In example 134, while the deletion and reversal of the units yields grammatical sentences, the resultant sentences are different in meaning than the original (example 134a):

(134a) *A Labour stalwart, Cllr Holtom* slated the council's previous Tory administration for causing "untold misery to the least fortunate." (SEU w.12.7k.4)
(134b) Cllr Holtom slated the council's previous Tory administration...
(134c) ?A Labour stalwart slated the council's previous Tory administration...
(134d) Cllr Holtom, a Labour stalwart, slated the council's previous Tory administration...

In example 134a, *A Labour stalwart* and *Cllr Holtom* are not units in apposition functioning as subject of the sentence. Rather, *A Labour stalwart* is a peripheral element, a noun phrase functioning as an adverbial. If *a Labour stalwart* were not an adverbial but the first unit of an apposition, we would expect, as Sopher (1971) and Quirk *et al.* (1985:1314–15) observe, a tone unit boundary or comma after the second unit (*Cllr Holtom*). In addition, *A Labour stalwart* has adverbial force in this example: it suggests not merely that Cllr Holtom is a Labour stalwart but that because he is a labour stalwart he slated the previous Tory administration. This meaning is lost if the units are deleted or reversed.

The units in example 135 are similar to those in example 134, except that the second unit in example 135 is even more clearly adverbial than *A Labour stalwart* in example 134. The unit *for many years a member of Weymouth to council* cannot stand alone or be reversed without syntactically ungrammatical examples resulting (examples 135b and d).

> (135a) *Mr. Hopkins, for many years a member of Weymouth to council*, built his house and garage from stone he cut from a private quarry. (SEU w.12.2.36)
> (135b) *For many years a member of Weymouth to council built his house…[with no intonation break after *years*]
> (135c) Mr. Hopkins built his house…
> (135d) *For many years a member of Weymouth to council, Mr. Hopkins, built his house…

2.5.4 *Apposition and modification*

There are two gradients involving apposition and modification: the gradient between apposition and premodification (see Figure 2.3) and the gradient between apposition and postmodification (see Figure 2.4).

2.5.4.1 *Apposition and premodification*

As Figure 2.3 illustrates, the gradient between apposition and pre-modification is a complex gradient: while the extremes of this gradient are easy to identify, intermediate cases have "fluid boundaries" (Bell 1988:330). At the modification end of the gradient are "institutionalized" titles (Quirk *et al.* 1985:1319), expressions such as *President* or *Professor* which precede a proper noun. Titles are typical premodifiers because they are structurally dependent on a head: they cannot stand alone (example 136c) or follow the head noun that they modify (example 136d).

> (136a) The board of regents of Paris Junior College has named *Dr. Clarence Charles Clark* of Hays, Kan. as the school's new president. (Brown A02 1530–50)
> (136b) …has named Charles Clark…
> (136c) *…has named Dr….
> (136d) *…has named Charles Clark, Dr….

Intermediate between apposition and modification are the "pseudo-titles" (Bell 1988) in examples 137 and 138. Like institutionalized titles, pseudo-titles cannot stand alone (the c examples below). However, like appositions,

Fig. 2.3 The gradient of apposition to premodification

Sentences:	a	b	c	d	e
Criteria					
1	+	+	+	+	+
2	+	?	−	−	−
3	+	+	+	−	−

Sentences
a My brother Joe was promoted to vice-president of the company.
b The novelist Graham Greene has always been politically active.
c Lobbyist Jane Jones was recently seen in Washington.
d Dr. Frank O'Connor was honored by the Medical Society of Boston.
e The extremely controversial "The Last Temptation of Christ" was banned in some American cities.

Criteria
1 The first unit of the apposition can be deleted.
2 The second unit of the apposition can be deleted.
3 The two units can be interchanged.

---

pseudo-titles and the nouns they precede can be interchanged (the d examples).

(137a) *Former Vice-President Richard M. Nixon* in Detroit called for a firmer and tougher policy toward the Soviet Union. (Brown A04 980–90)
(137b) ...Richard M. Nixon in Detroit called for...
(137c) *...Former Vice-President in Detroit called for...
(137d) ...Richard M. Nixon, former Vice-President, in Detroit called for...

(138a) *Trainer Jack Marsh*, of Eastchurch, Isle of Sheppey, found a capsule containing a fatal dose of phenobarbitone lying near one of his horses. (SEU w.12.2.12)
(138b) Jack Marsh...found a capsule...
(138c) *Trainer...found a capsule...
(138d) Jack Marsh, trainer,...found a capsule...

Example 137 illustrates the truly gradable nature of titles: while *Vice-President* is normally an institutionalized title, in this example it is converted into a pseudo-title.

At the apposition end of the gradient are the constructions in examples 139 and 140. The construction in example 139 is not completely appositional because the first unit of the construction is somewhat dependent for its meaning on the second unit and can therefore only awkwardly stand alone (example 139c).

> (139a) The village chosen is Wangala in Mandya District of Karnataka (formerly Mysore) State, which was studied by *the economist/anthropologist Scarlett Epstein* in 1955. (SEU w.9.6.31)
> (139b) ... which was studied by Scarlett Epstein ...
> (139c) ? ... which was studied by the economist/anthropologist ...
> (139d) ... which was studied by Scarlett Epstein, the economist/anthropologist.

Example 140 is fully appositional because the units in it satisfy all of the criteria for apposition.

> (140a) Houston was living at this time at Baron's Court in the flat which he shared with *his half-brother Hugh*, who was two years younger and a good deal noisier and rather inclined to take his shirts and his handkerchieves when he was home. (SEU w.16.7.25–1, 25–2)
> (140b) ... the flat which he shared with Hugh ...
> (140c) ... the flat which he shared with his half-brother ...
> (140d) ... the flat which he shared with Hugh, his half-brother ...

As the examples in this section illustrate, the main difference between apposition and premodification is the extent to which the first unit of the construction is structurally dependent on the second unit. If the units are in apposition, they will be structurally independent; if one unit modifies the other, only the head (and not the modifier) can stand alone and reversal of the units is not possible.

2.5.4.2 *Apposition and postmodification*

Figure 2.4 illustrates the gradient between apposition and postmodification. At the apposition end of the gradient is example 141, which satisfies all of the syntactic criteria for apposition.[13]

> (141a) *Robert Frost the poet* once spoke at the university.
> (141b) The poet once spoke at the university.
> (141c) Robert Frost once spoke at the university.
> (141d) The poet Robert Frost once spoke at the university.

Related to example 141 is example 142, a sentence containing units that are intermediate between apposition and postmodification. Like the units in example 141, those in example 142 can stand alone (the b and c examples). However, because the second unit in example 142 is structurally dependent

Fig. 2.4 The gradient of apposition to postmodification

Sentences:	a	b	c	d
Criteria				
1	+	+	−	−
2	+	+	+	+
3	+	−	−	−

Sentences

a Robert Frost the poet once spoke at the university.

b Eisenhower the man was different from Eisenhower the president.

c The possibility of a recession is real.

d The building that we work in caught fire last week.

Criteria

1 The first unit of the apposition can be deleted.

2 The second unit of the apposition can be deleted.

3 The two units can be interchanged.

to a degree on the first unit, the units in example 142, unlike those in example 141, cannot be interchanged (the d example).

> (142a) After they had finished eating, Mellisa took *Sprite the kitten* under her arm...(Brown N08 02–03)
> (142b) ...Mellisa took the kitten under her arm...
> (142c) ...Mellisa took Sprite under her arm...
> (142d) *...Mellisa took the kitten Sprite under her arm.

Towards the postmodification end of the gradient are the units in example 143. The second unit in this construction is quite structurally dependent on the first. As a result, the units in this example behave more like a head and modifier than an apposition. Like the second unit in example 144, which is a relative clause postmodifying a head noun, the second unit in example 143 cannot stand alone (the b example) and the units cannot be reversed (the d example). Only the first units in these structures can stand alone (the c examples).

> (143a) *The absolutely grotesque ritual* of *high table formal dinner in the evening* started with sherry. (LLC S.1.3 537–41)
> (143b) *Of high table formal dinner in the evening started...
> (143c) The absolutely grotesque ritual started...
> (143d) *...high table formal dinner in the evening of the absolutely grotesque ritual started...

(144a) It was in the middle of *this Dubrovniki Garden, which is a very overgrown kind of garden.* (LLC s.2.11 725–6)

(144b) *It was in the middle of which is a very overgrown kind of garden.

(144c) It was in the middle of this Dubrovniki Garden...

(144d) *It was in the middle of which is a very overgrown kind of garden, this Dubrovniki Garden.

Because the construction in example 143 behaves syntactically like a postmodifier, it is possible to say that *of* in this example is not an obligatory marker of apposition (2.1.3) but rather a preposition heading a prepositional phrase postmodifying a noun. However, the construction in example 143 is semantically appositional (3.1.1), making this construction a peripheral apposition.

Because the construction in example 145 has a relative clause paraphrase (example 146), constructions of this type have been regarded either as intermediate between apposition and modification (Matthews 1981:229–30) or as reduced relatives, a type of postmodifier (Burton-Roberts 1975).

(145) *Rep. Berry, an ex-gambler from San Antonio,* got elected on his advocacy of betting on the ponies. (Brown A02 620–30)

(146) Rep. Berry, who is an ex-gambler from San Antonio, got elected on his advocacy of betting on the ponies.

While constructions of the type in example 145 are semantically similar to other kinds of modifiers (3.1.2.2), syntactically the constructions are centrally appositional, since they fulfil all of the syntactic criteria for apposition:

(147a) An ex-gambler from San Antonio got elected...

(147b) Rep. Berry got elected...

(147c) An ex-gambler from San Antonio, Rep. Berry, got elected...

Consequently, the relationship between the constructions in examples 145 and 146 is one of correspondence (Greenbaum 1969:221f and Quirk *et al.* 1985:57) rather than of, say, gradience. That is to say, the construction in example 145 corresponds to (i.e. can be paraphrased by) a roughly synonymous construction having the form of a relative clause. The correspondence between apposition and other grammatical constructions is discussed in section 2.6.

2.5.5 *Apposition and complementation*

As Figure 2.5 demonstrates, the gradient between apposition and complementation involves constructions containing an initial unit that is a noun phrase and a second unit that is a clause beginning with *that* or *to*. No constructions of this type are centrally appositional. Consequently, the

Fig. 2.5 The gradient of apposition to complementation

Sentences:	a	b	c	d
Criteria				
1	+	−	−	−
2	+	+	+	+
3	?	?	−	−

Sentences

a The governor's contention that taxes need to be raised was disputed.
b The man's decision to drink and drive resulted in his having an accident.
c The attorney disagreed with the coroner's theory that the victim was not murdered.
d The president would not soothe our disappointment that U.S. troops were still in El Salvador.

Criteria

1 The first unit of the apposition can be deleted.
2 The second unit of the apposition can be deleted.
3 The two units can be interchanged.

gradient in Figure 2.5 is between peripheral apposition and complementation.

Examples 148 and 149 contain constructions that are intermediate between apposition and complementation. Because complementation is a relation in which the second unit is usually necessary to complete the meaning of the first unit (Quirk *et al.* 1985:65), the first unit of constructions on the gradient between apposition and complementation will not always be able to stand alone. In example 148, the first unit behaves somewhat appositionally, since it can stand alone (148c); in example 149, in contrast, the first unit (149c) is dependent on the second for its meaning and hence the relation between the units seems more like complementation than apposition.

> (148a) *The suggestion that we should put you down, demolish you, and rebuild you* is obviously not going to make much impression on that [the excessive amount of noise created by construction crews]. (LLC s.3.4 286–9)
> (148b) ?That we should put you down, demolish you, and rebuild you is obviously not going to make much impression on that.

(148c) The suggestion is obviously not going to make much impression on that.

(148d) ?That we should put you down, demolish you, and rebuild you, the suggestion, is obviously not going to make much impression on that.

(149a) What they will probably come up with is *the proposal that we put all of the texts in this onto a cassette tape.* (LLC s.3.2 892–6)

(149b) What they will probably come up with is that we put all of the texts onto a cassette tape.

(149c) ?What they will probably come up with is the proposal.

(149d) ?What they will probably come up with is that we put all of the texts onto a cassette tape, the proposal.

But even though the first unit in example 149 cannot stand alone, the construction does behave somewhat appositionally because the second unit can stand alone (example 149b). Furthermore, the units in example 149 are clearly distinguishable from those in example 150, a construction whose second unit seems more like a complement of the first than the second unit of an apposition. Because the valency of the verb *approve* prohibits an object having the form of a *to*-infinitive, the second unit cannot stand alone (the b example) and the units cannot be reversed (the d example).

(150a) Sikhs meeting in London yesterday approved *a plan to try to suppress publication of future immigration speeches by Mr Enoch Powell.* (SEU w.12.3f–1)

(150b) *Sikhs meeting in London yesterday approved to try...

(150c) Sikhs meeting in London yesterday approved a plan...

(150d) *Sikhs meeting in London yesterday approved to try to suppress publication of future immigration speeches by Mr Enoch Powell, a plan...

Because the second unit in example 150 behaves so much like a complement of the noun that precedes it, it would appear that the relationship between the units in this example is one of complementation rather than apposition. However, the construction in example 150 differs from other instances of noun complementation in three respects. First, as Matthews (1981:231) observes, the first unit in constructions such as the above can be separated from the second unit by a tone unit boundary, yielding an instance of nonrestrictive apposition (3.3). In the example below, the tone unit boundary is marked by the comma after *point*:

(151) Combellack argues further, and here he makes *his main point, that once the Illiad and the Odyssey are thought formulaic poetry, Homeric critics are deprived of an entire domain they previously found arable.* (Brown j67 086–90)

No other noun complements, as Matthews notes, permit the restrictive and nonrestrictive oppositions illustrated in example 151 and the examples in this section preceding it. Second, constructions such as the one in example 150 have the same correspondences that other appositions have (2.6). Specifically, constructions of the type in example 150 correspond to constructions containing subject complements. In example 152, for instance, the noun *fact*, which occurs quite commonly in appositions of this type (2.1.2), can head a noun phrase functioning as the subject of a sentence containing a *that*-clause as subject complement.

> (152) An interesting fact is that Jeyes' chairman, Mr. Stephen Steen, is also deputy-chairman and executive chief of Smith and Nephew. (SEU w.12.6a–2)

Noun complements have no correspondence to sentences containing subject complements. In example 153a, a copular relationship does not exist between the noun phrase *an attempt* and the *to*-clause that is its complement (example 153b).

> (153a) *An attempt to improve the life of the anodes or the efficiency of the plasma generators* must, therefore, aim at a reduction of the anode loss. (Brown J02 450–80)
>
> (153b) *An attempt was to improve the life of the anodes...

Finally, constructions such as those in example 150 are semantically similar to other kinds of appositions (3.1.1.3), providing further evidence of the difference between instances of complementation (example 153) and instances of peripheral apposition (examples 148–150).

2.6 Systematic correspondences between appositions and other grammatical constructions

Quirk *et al.* (1985:57) define systematic correspondence "as a relation or mapping between two structures X and Y, such that if the same lexical content occurs in X and in Y, there is a constant meaning relation between the two structures." In English, sentences in the active voice correspond systematically to equivalent sentences in the passive voice. The passive sentence *The dog was walked by John* has the same meaning as its active equivalent (*John walked the dog*), and is derived from it through systematic structural changes. With appositions, we find similar systematic correspondences: between appositions and relative clauses and subject complements, and (to a lesser extent) between appositions and certain types of verb-complement constructions.

2.6.1 *Appositions and relative clauses and subject complements*

Because of the relationship between nonrestrictive relative clauses and appositions, a number of sources, as Matthews (1981:229) notes, regard nonrestrictive relative clauses as appositive relative clauses. However, as Burton-Roberts (1975) rightly observes, not all appositions have relative clause correspondences. An apposition will systematically correspond to a relative clause only if a copular relation exists between the two units in the apposition. That is to say, in order for an apposition to have a relative clause paraphrase, the two units must be able to occur in sentences in which the first unit is subject and the second unit subject complement. Consequently, there is a close systematic correspondence between appositions, subject/ subject complement constructions, and nonrestrictive relative clauses.

This correspondence is illustrated in examples 154 and 155. In each of these examples, there is a correspondence between an apposition (the a examples), a relative clause (the b examples), and a construction containing a subject and subject complement (the c examples):

(154a) He had therefore concurred with *the abbot's plan, to merely say nothing until requests for information came from Lhasa; and then to announce that the party was missing.*

(154b) He had therefore concurred with the abbot's plan, which was merely to say nothing until requests for information came from Lhasa; and then to announce that the party was missing. (SEU w.16.7.136–3)

(154c) He had therefore concurred with the abbot's plan. The plan was to say nothing until requests for information came from Lhasa; and then to announce that the party was missing.

(155a) There is also, in the larva, a tissue known as *muco-cartilage, an elastic material serving more as an antagonist to the muscles than for their attachment.*

(155b) There is also, in the larva, a tissue known as muco-cartilage, which is an elastic material serving more as an antagonist to the muscles than for their attachment. (SEU w.9.7.85–2)

(155c) There is also, in the larva, a tissue known as muco-cartilage. Muco-cartilage is an elastic material serving more as an antagonist to the muscles than for their attachment.

These kinds of systematic correspondences are ruled out, however, if there is no copular relationship between the first unit of an apposition and the second unit. In example 156, because the units cannot occur as subject and subject complement (the c example), a relative clause paraphrase is not possible (the b example).

(156a) Like Herbert, they were all in *communications: radio, television, magazines, and advertising.* (Brown R02 1330–40)

(156b) *Like Herbert, they were all in communications, which are radio, television, magazines, and advertising.

(156c) *Communications are radio, television, magazines, and advertising.

2.6.2 *Appositions and verb-complement constructions*

Some appositions consist of a first unit that is a nominalized noun phrase and a second unit that is a *that-* or *to-*clause (2.1.2). Appositions of this type have correspondences to constructions containing the verbal equivalent of the nominalized noun followed by the *that-* or *to-*clause. Example 157 illustrates this correspondence with a *that-*clause, example 158 with a *to-*clause:

> (157a) He had *a lowering feeling that he had somehow missed the bus, that some of the virtue had gone out of him in the past year.* (SEU w.16.7.26–4)
> (157b) He felt that he had somehow missed the bus, that some of the virtue had gone out of him in the past year.

> (158a) He told the crowded meeting of *his decision to carry on,* for the best interests of party and country. (SEU w.12.2.5)
> (158b) He told the crowded meeting that he had decided to carry on, for the best interests of party and country.

Correspondences of this kind, however, are not as systematic as those between appositions and relative clauses and subject complements. While the apposition in example 159a corresponds to an entire sentence (159b), this corresponding sentence does not fit syntactically into the structure of the entire sentence containing the apposition (159c):

> (159a) This has an interesting analogy with *the assumption stated by Philippoff that "the deformational mechanics of elastic solids can be applied to flowing solutions."* (Brown J03 950–80)
> (159b) Philippoff assumed that "the deformational mechanics of elastic solids can be applied to flowing solutions."
> (159c) *This has an interesting analogy with Philippoff assumed that "the deformational mechanics of elastic solids can be applied to flowing solutions."

3 The semantics of apposition

In the previous chapter, the relation of apposition was discussed in terms of the syntactic characteristics that typify the units of an apposition. In this chapter, the focus shifts from the syntactic structure of units in apposition to their semantic structure.

The semantic relationship between units in apposition can be described in a variety of ways. The two units of an apposition can be characterized by the semantic relations existing between them, relations that are either referential (3.1.1) or non-referential (3.1.2). In addition, appositions can be classified into various semantic classes, depending upon whether the second unit of the apposition provides information about the first that is more specific (3.2.1), less specific (3.2.2), or equally specific (3.2.3). In appositions containing first units that are noun phrases, the apposition can be categorized according to whether or not the second unit of the apposition restricts the reference of the first unit (3.3). And finally, appositions form semantic gradients (3.4), with some appositions being semantically more appositional than others.

3.1 The semantic relations between units in apposition

Traditionally, apposition has been considered a relation consisting of two units that are coreferential (cf., for instance, Fries 1952:187, Hockett 1955:101, Quirk et al. 1985:1301, and Burton-Roberts 1975). However, as is argued in Meyer (1987a), not all constructions considered appositions in the literature consist of units that are coreferential, and to restrict the relation of apposition to only those constructions whose units are coreferential severely limits the number of constructions that can be admitted as appositions. A much more desirable alternative, it is argued in Meyer (1987a), is to expand the number of semantic relations holding between units in apposition in order to admit as appositions a variety of different constructions.

Table 3.1 outlines the semantic relations needed to account for all constructions that are considered appositions in this study. As Table 3.1 demonstrates, the vast majority of appositions (62 percent) contained units

Table 3.1. *Semantic relationships between units in apposition*

Relationship	Brown	LLC	SEU	Total
Reference				
Coreference	365	263	469	1,097
Part/whole	64	90	78	232
Cataphoric reference	154	111	162	427
Total	583	464	709	1,756 (62%)
Synonymy				
Absolute	26	16	34	76
Speaker	53	47	35	135
Clausal	87	195	74	356
Total	166	258	143	567 (20%)
Attribution				
Phrasal	238	15	153	406
Clausal/phrasal	12	2	15	29
Total	250	17	168	435 (15%)
Hyponymy				
Syntagmatic	20	30	7	57
Non-syntagmatic	7	9	10	26
Total	27	39	17	83 (3%)
Total	1,026	778	1,037	2,841 (100%)

related by some kind of referential relation: coreference, part/whole reference, or cataphoric reference. Far fewer appositions (38 percent) contained units related by the nonreferential relations of synonymy, attribution, or hyponymy.

3.1.1 *Referential relations between units in apposition*

Table 3.2 provides a detailed breakdown of the various kinds of referential relations that can exist between units in apposition. The two units of an apposition can be coreferential; that is, they can "refer to the same 'piece of reality'" (Leech 1981:156):

> (1) Not many days elapsed before a stranger wrote to say that at the suggestion of *his friend*, *Mr Alexander Goodrich*, he was asking Harold to take charge of his income-tax return. (SEU w.16.5.18–2)

Alternatively, the reference of the second unit of the apposition can be included within the reference of the first unit, resulting in a part/whole relation (Lyons 1977:311) between the units:

Table 3.2. *Referential relations between units in apposition*

Relation	Brown	LLC	SEU	Total
Coreference				
NPs	360	199	457	1,016
Place adv	2	4	4	10
Time adv	3	0	2	5
Total	365	203	463	1,031 (59%)
Speaker coreference				
with *or*	0	37	5	42
without *or*	0	23	1	24
Total	0	60	6	66 (4%)
Part/whole reference	64	90	78	232 (13%)
Cataphoric reference				
to clauses	112	91	146	349
to sentences	42	20	16	78
Total	154	111	162	427 (24%)
Total	583	464	709	1,756 (100%)

(2) I haven't heard from them, but I think I was never at all in the running. They had, they shortlisted *five people*, including *me*. (LLC s.1.3 251–5)

Finally, if the second unit is not a referring expression (as the interrogative sentence in example 3 is not [3.1.1.3]), the first unit of the apposition can simply refer cataphorically to the second unit:

(3) The *Sane Society* is an ambitious work. Its scope is as broad as *the question*: *What does it mean to live in modern society?* (Brown J62 010–20)

As Table 3.2. indicates, these three relations did not occur with equal frequency in the corpora. The majority of appositions (63 percent) contained units that were coreferential; far fewer consisted of a first unit referring cataphorically to a second unit (24 percent) or a second unit whose reference was included within the reference of the first unit (13 percent).

3.1.1.1 *Coreferential relations between units in apposition*
As Table 3.2 illustrates, the units of an apposition can exhibit either strict coreference or speaker coreference. These two types of coreference are distinguished by the extent to which the meaning of the items that corefer parallel their referents (Akmajian *et al.* 1984:244–5). In the apposition in

example 4 below, the units are strictly coreferential because there is a close connection between the meaning of the units and the referents in the external world that they refer to.

> (4) A pastoral letter from *the Bishop of Bristol, Dr. Tomkins,* was read today in churches throughout the diocese. (SEU w.12.1–48)

In contrast, in the apposition in example 5, the units have distinct meanings and ought therefore to have different referents. However, because the speaker of this utterance intends the words to have the same extralinguistic reference, the notion of speaker coreference (see Donnellan 1979) has been postulated to capture the coreference inherent in such examples.

> (5) There's a chapter on *the aesthetics of Piggott,* or, or *an aesthetic of Piggott.* (LLC s.3.6 491–2)

Strict coreference, as Table 3.2 demonstrates, was the most common kind of reference that occurred in the corpora; speaker coreference occurred quite rarely and almost solely in the spoken corpus.

Strict coreference is a relation that can exist between three kinds of referring expressions in English: place adverbials, time adverbials, and certain types of noun phrases (Lyons 1977: 660).[1] As Table 3.2 shows, appositions containing coreferential place adverbials (example 6) and time adverbials (example 7) were rare in the corpora:

> (6) They lie *on either side of the spinal cord* (Fig. 50), that is to say, *above the notochord,* and consist either of one nodule on each side of the segment, through the middle of which the ventral nerve-root emerges, or of two separate nodules, with the nerve between them. (SEU w9.7.86–1, 87–1)

> (7) AT LEAST six Camden secondary schools and most local primary schools were closed *yesterday* (*Wednesday*) as a result of a one-day national strike by the National Union of Teachers in support of a pay claim. (SEU w.12.7d.2)

It was much more common for appositions to contain coreferential noun phrases. These noun phrases may have a variety of different referents, including individuals (example 8), objects (example 9), and abstractions (example 10).[2]

> (8) Linda dragooned *her uncle, Donald Murkland,* into a lunch the next day to find out what had happened. (Brown P17 1440–50)

> (9) An anonymous letter-writer who has lost his job is threatening to burn down a church in retaliation for his

misfortunes. *The church, St. Michael's and All Saints, Pelsall, Staffs,* has been closed, except for services, until police find the author. (SEU w.12.2.39)

(10) He had *an easy masculine grace* about him, *the kind that kids don't have, but that I had sometimes admired in other older men.* (Brown P22 320–40)

Speaker coreference is a relation occurring in two types of constructions: juxtaposed noun phrases (example 11) or noun phrases joined by the marker of apposition *or* and followed optionally by the conjunct *rather* (example 12).

(11) This *Mr Mifuno,* no, *Mr Ayto,* sorry, Mr Ayto was from, from their Russian section. (LLC s.2.11 1171–6)

(12) Colonel Nasser and King Hussein have certainly gone further to accommodate King Faisal's ruthless logic and *they,* or rather *their State-controlled presses,* have long been saying, in so many words, that the mission is dead. (SEU w.12.3b–3)

Although the constructions in examples (11) and (12) can be admitted as appositions because their units are coreferential, these constructions differ from other appositions in two respects. First, the constructions in each of these examples can be analyzed as performance errors rather than appositions: they fit within Garnham *et al.*'s (1982) class of semantic substitutions, words added to the discourse to correct a previously chosen word not reflecting the meaning the speaker intended. Second, although *or* in example 12 is regarded in this study as a marker of apposition, it can also be considered an instance of interpolated coordination which Quirk *et al.* (1985:933) term corrective *or.* This use of *or* is not restricted to joining noun phrases such as those in example 12, but occurs freely in other kinds of constructions that are clearly not in apposition. Although clauses can be in apposition if they are synonymous (3.1.2.1), the clauses joined by *or* in example 13 are not synonymous and therefore not in apposition.

(13) They are enjoying themselves, *or (at least)/(rather)* they appear to be enjoying themselves. [italics in original]

Because constructions such as those in examples 11 and 12 have multiple analyses, they must be considered questionable instances of apposition.

3.1.1.2 *Part/whole relations between units in apposition*
In appositions whose units are coreferential there is an exact correspondence between the units and their referents. In other appositions, however, there is not an exact correspondence between the units and their referents. Instead, the reference of the second unit is included within the reference of

the first unit, a type of semantic relation that Lyons (1977:311) terms a "part/whole" relation. Examples 14 and 15 illustrate this relation. In example 14, the particular agency described in the second unit of the apposition is one member of the class of multipurpose agencies mentioned in the first unit.

> (14) Increased experimentation with *multipurpose agencies, especially those that combine afresh the traditional functions of family and child welfare services*, holds rich promise for the future. (Brown J24 1940–70)

In example 15, the individual mentioned in the second unit of the apposition (*Ludendorff*) is a member of the class of people referred to in the first unit.

> (15) There were plenty of aristocrats, even in the great General staff, but there were *plenty of people* like *Ludendorff* who had absolutely no kind of family or anything. (LLC s.2.3 190–3)

Appositions such as those in examples 14 and 15 typically contain first units that are indefinite and plural and second units that are definite (2.1.3.1). These syntactic characteristics create an apposition in which the first unit is more general than the second unit, and in which an obligatory marker of apposition is therefore required to explicitly mark the part/whole relation existing between the units. In the corpora, the most frequently occurring markers were *such as, like, including, especially, particular*, and *in particular* (see Table 2.16). Markers such as these are necessary because if they are lacking in the apposition, the part/whole relation between the units will change in one of three ways. First, the construction in which the apposition occurs will change in meaning. If the marker is removed from example 14, the units will be interpreted as coreferential, and the second unit will become not an instance of one multipurpose organization but the only organization of this type referred to in the example:

> (16) Increased experimentation with multipurpose organiza- tions, those that combine afresh the traditional functions of family and child welfare services, holds rich promise for the future.

Second, in other appositions (such as the apposition in example 15), removal of the marker results in a semantically implausible sentence that is ungrammatical:

> (17) *...there were plenty of people, Ludendorff, who had absolutely no family or anything.

Finally, absence of a marker results in ambiguities, particularly if the second unit contains an asyndetically coordinated series. In example 18, it is not clear whether the units are coreferential or inclusively coreferential; that is, whether the second unit of the apposition provides an exhaustive list of everything the individuals needed to start a new life, or merely representative examples.

> (18) Already some of the pain had gone from Amelia's death. Not all of it. There would still be plenty of moments of regret and sadness and guilty relief. But they were starting a new life. And they had *almost everything they needed: land, a house, two whiteface bulls, three horses.* (Brown N05 1220–60)

Because a part/whole interpretation is possible in sentences such as 18, Quirk *et al.* (1985:1315) remark that a marker of apposition is not always necessary in some kinds of appositions whose units are in a part/whole relation to one another. However, as examples 16–18 demonstrate, a marker is quite necessary in order to clearly and unambiguously mark the semantic relation of inclusion existing between the units of these kinds of appositions.

3.1.1.3 *Appositions in which the first unit refers cataphorically to the second unit*

The appositions in the previous two sections contained units that could both refer: noun phrases and temporal and locative adverbials. Some appositions, however, consist of units that cannot both refer. In example 19, for instance, the first unit is a definite noun phrase and can therefore refer. However, because the second unit is a clause, it has no referring value.

> (19) If barbarous nations have been barbarous because it was their nature so to be, then, if they become independent, they will slowly or quickly sink back into barbarism, and it is no good acting on *the assumption that they will do anything else.* (SEU W.9.3.5–1)

To account for the relation between the units in appositions such as 19, we need to distinguish, as Cornish (1986:10) argues, between two types of anaphoric and cataphoric reference: reference between constructions which are also coreferential and reference between constructions which are not coreferential.[3]

The difference between the two types of reference is illustrated in examples 20 and 21. Example 20 contains an apposition whose units exhibit anaphora and coreference: because the second unit is definite and the first unit indefinite, the second unit refers anaphorically to the first unit; in turn, the two units are coreferential because they have identical referents.

> (20) Ramsey has a thing or two to mutter about himself, for the Dallas defensive unit turned in another splendid effort against

Denver, and the Texans were able to whip the dangerous Broncs without the fullbacking of *a top star, Jack Spikes*, though he did the team's place-kicking while nursing a knee injury. (Brown A12 1410–50)

Example 21, on the other hand, contains an apposition whose units exhibit cataphora but not coreference: the first unit is a definite noun phrase that refers cataphorically to the second unit; however, the two units are not coreferential because the second unit is a clause and therefore has no referring value.[4]

(21) United in a refusal to make a legal rate[,] the hard-line London councils could present a formidable political challenge; much will hinge, for both the Labour Party and the Government, on *Mr Kinnock's bid to make Labour responsible and Labour councillors more aware of their responsibilities*. (SEU w.12.8m.9)

To account for the semantic relation between the units in appositions such as those in examples 19 and 21, we need to add a third referential relation between units in apposition, namely that in appositions of this type, the first unit refers cataphorically to the second unit.

Cataphoric reference of the first unit of the apposition to the second unit occurs in any apposition in which the first unit is a noun phrase and the second unit a clause or sentence (see 2.1.2 and 2.1.3.2). In examples 22 and 23, the initial units consist of noun phrases that refer cataphorically to clauses.

(22) *This* is what Rivens wanted: *to introduce course one into Refford*. (LLC s.1.6 651–2)

(23) No word exists that refers exclusively to *the phenomenon* of *bright light striking a particular small area of a reflecting surface and seeming to blaze or burn in the object it strikes*. (SEU w.9.4.60–1)

In examples 24 and 25, the initial units refer cataphorically to entire sentences.

(24) All lampreys have a life-history that includes *two distinct stages: the ammocoete larva lives in fresh water, buried in the mud, and is microphagous; the adult lamprey has a sucking mouth, and usually lives in the sea, where it feeds on other fishes*. (SEU w.9.7.83–1)

(25) The largest hurdle the Republicans would have to face is a state law which says that before making a first race, *one of two alternative courses* must be taken:

Table 3.3. *Non-referential relations between units in apposition: synonymy*

Type of synonymy	Brown	LLC	SEU	Total
Absolute	26	16	34	76 (13%)
Speaker	53	47	35	135 (24%)
Clausal/sentential	87	195	74	356 (63%)
Total	166	258	143	567 (100%)

1. *Five per cent of the voters in each county must sign petitions requesting that the Republicans be allowed to place names of candidates on the general election ballot, or*
2. *The Republicans must hold a primary under the county unit system – a system which the party opposes in its platform.* (Brown A01 1000–60)

3.1.2 *Non-referential relations between units in apposition*

As Table 3.1 indicates, the majority of the appositions in the corpora (62 percent) contained units related referentially. The remaining appositions (38 per cent) were related by the non-referential relations of synonymy, attribution, and hyponymy. Most of these appositions (35 percent) contained units related by the relations of synonymy and attribution; far fewer (only 3 percent) were comprised of units related by the relation of hyponymy.

3.1.2.1 *Appositions whose units are synonymous*
Table 3.3 outlines the frequency of occurrence of the three kinds of synonymy that existed between the units of appositions in the corpora. Approximately two-thirds (63 percent) of the appositions in this category consisted of units that were synonymous clauses or sentences; the remaining appositions (37 percent) contained units exhibiting two kinds of lexical synonymy: absolute synonymy and speaker synonymy.

Lexical synonymy, as Cruse (1986:265) observes, is a matter of degree: "some pairs of synonyms are more 'synonymous' than other pairs..." This view of synonymy quite accurately describes the relationship between the units of appositions that are synonyms, since such units exhibit varying degrees of synonymy. In examples 26–30, there is "absolute" synonymy between the units in apposition: the units, as Cruse (1986:268) notes, have identical meanings because their "contextual relations" (i.e. their meanings in any contexts) would be identical. Absolute synonymy, as Table 3.4 indicates, was most frequently a relation between units that were noun phrases, and less commonly a relation between units of other form classes.

Table 3.4. *Forms of absolute synonyms*

Form	Brown	LLC	SEU	Total
NP + NP	17	8	19	44 (58%)
Adj ph + adj ph	4	6	7	17 (22%)
VP + VP	2	1	1	4
Prep ph + prep ph	0	0	4	4
Adv ph + adv ph	2	0	0	2
Other	1	1	3	5
Total	26	16	34	76

In appositions whose units were synonymous noun phrases, the noun phrases were indefinite or generic and occurred in two contexts: as juxtaposed noun phrases (example 26) or (less commonly) as noun phrases functioning as objects of prepositions within prepositional phrases in apposition (example 27):

> (26) Call it what you like. Call it nationalism, or call it *decentralization, re-organization of local government*, something along those lines. (LLC s.2.8 200–5)

> (27) In order to present a concept as an object we should have to introduce the concept by means of a substantival expression; but Frege wishes to think of a concept as essentially something that can be represented *only* [italics in original] by *a nonsubstantival expression*, by *an expression that introduces its term in the verb-like, coupling, propositional style.* (SEU W.9.1.152–2)

In appositions whose units were not noun phrases, the units were most frequently adjective phrases (example 28) and much less frequently verb phrases (example 29) or adverb phrases (example 30).

> (28) This circumstance in the patient's case plus the fact that his tactual capacity remained basically in sound working order constitutes its exceptional value for the problem at hand since the evidence presented by the authors is overwhelming that, when the patient closed his eyes, he had absolutely no *spatial* (that is *third-dimensional*) awareness whatsoever. (Brown J52 100–50)

> (29) *The Evening News* was *finished, consumed.* (SEU W.16.4.53–2)

> (30) It snowed *softly, silently*, an undulating interruption of his vision against the night sky. (Brown L06 980–90)

Table 3.5. *Forms of speaker synonyms*

Form	Brown	LLC	SEU	Total
NP + NP	40	27	28	95 (70%)
Adj ph + adj ph	6	9	1	16 (12%)
Prep ph + prep ph	2	5	3	10
VP + VP	2	0	0	2
Adv ph + adv ph	0	1	0	1
Other	3	5	5	11
Total	53	47	35	135

At the other end of the scale of synonymy are words which exhibit "speaker" synonymy. That is to say, the words are not synonymous in the dictionary sense but rather in the sense that the speaker intends them to be synonymous. One of the words in this type of synonymy, Cruse (1986:267) maintains, serves "as an explanation, or clarification, of the meaning of another word." In appositions whose units exhibit a relation of speaker synonymy, the function of explanation is provided by the second unit of the apposition, which instead of providing an exact paraphrase of the first unit, clarifies its meaning instead. In example 31, for instance, the two units are not absolute synonyms; instead, the second unit provides an explanation (or definition) of what the speaker means by *three duds* in the first unit.

(31) You might actually get *three duds*, I mean, *three people whom you didn't want*. (LLC s.2.6 477–8)

As Table 3.5 illustrates, appositions whose units were speaker synonyms occurred more frequently than those whose units were absolute synonyms. However, like units that were absolute synonyms, those that were speaker synonyms tended most frequently to be indefinite or generic noun phrases such as those in examples 31 and 32.

(32) It [the inspiration of the Old Testament] was *an inspiration with prophetic importance: a pointing to the last days when God would speak by His Son*. (SEU w.9.2.136–3)

It was less common for the units to be adjective phrases (example 33), verb phrases (example 34), or adverb phrases (example 35).

(33) It [the beer] tasted *so watery*, you know, *lifeless*. (LLC s.1.7 239–40)

(34) He felt *depressed, flattened*. (SEU w.1.16.6.170–3)

(35) The Government's ratecapping legislation derives from pure and simple frustration. It has watched in helpless rage

Table 3.6. *Forms of clausal synonyms*

Form	Brown	LLC	SEU	Total
Predications	8	16	9	33 (9%)
Subordinate clauses	20	20	24	64 (18%)
Sentences	59	159	41	259 (73%)
Total	87	195	74	356 (100%)

> while the GLC, and some of the local councils such as Islington, have spent *recklessly*, *profligately*, on public relations departments, race relations committees, women's liaison groups and so on. (SEU w.12.8h.1–2)

The notions of absolute and speaker synonymy provide a useful way of describing the varying degrees of synonymy in appositions whose units are phrases. In appositions whose units are clauses, however, such notions are of little use. To account for the synonymy of clauses rather than words, it is necessary to move from lexical semantics to truth functional semantics. Within truth functional semantics, there is one truth function that can be used to describe clausal synonymy: the notion that clauses will be synonymous if they express the same truth value. According to Leech (1981:74), the units X and Y will be synonymous if "X has the same truth value as Y; i.e. if X is true, Y is true; also if X is false, Y is false; and vice versa." In the corpora, this formula was used to identify as appositions constructions consisting of two units that were clauses (2.1.4.2). In example 36a, for instance, the units (which are sentences) are synonymous and hence in apposition because they express the same truth value: the truth of the first unit insures the truth of the second; in turn, the falsity of the first unit insures the falsity of the second unit, since (as example 36b illustrates) if the train were not full it would not be nearly completely reserved.

> (36a) [The] train was nearly full: [that is to say] it was nearly all reserved. (LLC s.1.6 602–3)
> (36b) [The] train was not nearly full: [that is to say] it was not nearly all reserved.

Table 3.6 lists the three kinds of constructions whose units could be related by the relation of clausal synonymy. It was most common, as Table 3.6 illustrates, for the units to be sentences (example 37).

> (37) And he [the patient] could recognize, by touch alone, articles which he had handled immediately before, even though they were altogether unfamiliar to him and could not be

identified by him; that is, he was unaware what kinds of objects they were or what their use was. (Brown J53 650–80)

However, the units could also be a subordinate clause, such as the *to*-infinitive clauses in example 38 or the *if*-clauses in example 39; or they could be a predicate phrase (2.1.4.1), as in example 40.

(38) Once or twice he made as if *to move*, [that is to say] *to get up and stretch his legs, go for a drink in the bar, walk outside and take a look at the sky and the pigeons and taxi-cabs*, but in the end he did not, he simply sat, watching. (SEU w.16.8.8–9)

(39) If goodness and badness lie in attitudes only and hence are brought into being by them, those men who greeted death and misery with childishly merry laughter are taking the only sensible line. *If there is nothing evil in these things*, [that is to say] *if they get their moral complexion only from our feeling about them*, why shouldn't they be greeted with a cheer? (Brown J52 1500–50)

(40) I had a seminar today in which people *hadn't read the stuff because of sessionals*, [that is to say] *hadn't read the play*, so we had to spin it out. (LLC s.1.4 1081–5)

3.1.2.2 *Appositions whose units are related by the relation of attribution*

Occurring slightly less frequently than appositions whose units are synonyms are appositions whose units are related by the relation of attribution. This relation, as Table 3.1 demonstrates, accounted for 15 percent of the appositions in the corpora.

In attributive appositions, one of the units is a non-referring noun phrase that has an "ascriptive, descriptive or classificatory role" (Burton-Roberts 1975:395) in relation to the other unit of the apposition with which it occurs. In example 41, for instance, because the second unit of the apposition is a noun phrase containing an attributive indefinite article (see Burton-Roberts 1976:427 and 2.1.1.2), the noun phrase has no referring value (Quirk *et al.* 1985:273); instead, it attributes a particular characteristic to the first unit, namely that the individual referred to in the first unit has the characteristic of being a lifelong teetotaler.

(41) The jail authorities – attaching no particular significance to the episode – offered Barco whisky to revive him; but *the old fellow*, *a lifelong teetotaler*, refused it, and no more was thought of the matter. (Brown R01 320–50)

As Table 3.7 indicates, most attributive appositions occurred in the written samples of the corpora, particularly in the samples from the Brown Corpus; virtually no appositions of this type occurred in the spoken samples. This

Table 3.7. *Non referential relations between units in apposition: attribution*

Form	Brown	LLC	SEU	Total
NP (−det) + proper NP	97	1	31	129 (30%)
Proper NP + NP (−det)	65	0	56	121 (28%)
Proper NP + NP (i/a)	42	4	35	81 (19%)
Misc NP + NP (i/a)	27	8	21	56 (13%)
Sent/clause + NP (i/a)	12	2	15	29 (7%)
NP (i) + NP (i/a)	7	2	10	19 (4%)
Total	250	17	168	435 (100%)

i = indefinite
i/a = indefinite/attributive
−det = NP lacking determiner

skewed distribution has a pragmatic explanation (4.4.2.3): in spontaneous conversation, speakers will generally have prior knowledge of the noun phrases that they introduce into the discourse and therefore will not need to attribute characteristics to them.

As Table 3.7 also points out, attributive appositions had a variety of different forms. The majority of such appositions (58 percent) contained either an initial unit (example 42) or a second unit (example 43) lacking a determiner and therefore having no referring value (Ziff 1960:113).

> (42) Two errors by *New York Yankee shortshop Tony Kubek* in the eleventh inning donated four unearned runs and a 5-to-2 victory to the Chicago White Sox today. (Brown A11 1840–60)

> (43) LORD BLAKENHAM, *chairman of the party*, said that he sensed growing confidence and determination in Conservative ranks. (SEU w.12.1–24, 1–25)

The remaining appositions contained non-referring second units that attributed characteristics to a variety of different forms in the first unit. In example 44, the second unit attributes to the individual in the first unit the characteristic of being a member of the Conservative party.

> (44) In May, shortly before the municipal elections, *Councillor Donald Finney, a Conservative*, alleged that Spon Lane was a centre of vice. (SEU w.12.1–6)

In example 45, the second unit follows a definite noun phrase and classifies the referent of the noun phrase as being in the class of women disliked by one of the characters in the passage.

> (45) Houston didn't blame him. He knew that if he wanted, Hugh would stop frittering his money and keep him in turn. He could give the sailor's farewell to *the Head of the Edith Road*

Girls' Secondary, a woman he deplored, and on any propitious day set up as an artist. (SEU w.16.7.26–4)

In example 46, the second unit follows an indefinite first unit. Because both units are indefinite, appositions of this type seem similar to those whose units are synonyms (3.1.2.1). However, the second unit in example 46, unlike the second unit of an apposition whose units are synonyms, does not provide an exact paraphrase of the first unit. Rather, it attributes to the total offense mentioned in the first unit the characteristic of being a conference record.

> (46) Texas' 545–yard spree against Washington State gave the Longhorns *a 3-game total offense of 1,512 yards (1,065 rushing and 447 passing), a new SWC high.* (Brown A11 1680–90)

In example 47, the second unit follows a first unit that is not a noun phrase but an entire clause or sentence. The second unit in this kind of apposition, termed a "summative modifier" by Williams (1979:609), first summarizes the ideas expressed in the first unit and then attributes some characteristic to them. In example 47, the first part of the second unit, *a process,* provides a very general summary of the activity of decomposition discussed in the first unit; the relative clause following this noun phrase characterizes this process as one that occurs more rapidly in a specific environment.

> (47) These micro-organisms decompose organic matter in the soil and release plant nutrients, a process which occurs particularly rapidly in an oxidised soil under tropical conditions of warmth and humidity. (SEU w.9.6.18)

3.1.2.3 *Appositions whose units are related by the relation of hyponymy*
Appositions related by the relation of hyponymy were, as Table 3.1 indicates, the least frequently occurring appositions in the corpora: only 3 percent of the appositions contained a second unit that was a hyponym of the first unit.

Hyponymous appositions can be characterized in two ways. First, because the second unit of such appositions is a hyponym of the first unit, a relation of "meaning inclusion" (Leech 1981:92) exists between the two units: the meaning of the second unit is included within the more general meaning of the first unit. In example 48, because the second unit (*dead roots and shoots, manure, soil humus…*) is more specific than the first unit (*organic matter*), the semantic features needed to characterize *organic matter* (e.g. +animate, −human) would be two of the many features needed to characterize the meaning of the more specific second unit.

> (48) The nitrogen in *organic matter (dead roots and shoots, manure, soil humus, etc.)* is changed during decomposition to an ammonium form…(SEU w.9.6.19)

Table 3.8. *Non-referential relations between units in apposition: hyponymy*

Form	Brown	LLC	SEU	Total
Different heads				
NP	6	7	9	22 (27%)
Non-NP	1	2	1	4 (5%)
Syntagmatic				
NP	14	25	6	45 (54%)
Non-NP	6	5	1	12 (14%)
Total	27	39	17	83 (100%)

Second, because of the superordinate/subordinate meaning relationship
existing between the units, the second unit stands in a "kind of" relation
(Lyons 1977:292) to the first unit: *dead roots, manure,* and *soil humus* in the
apposition in example 48 can be regarded as "kinds of" *organic matter.*[5]

As Table 3.8 indicates, most hyponymous appositions in the corpora (81
percent) consisted of units that were noun phrases. These noun phrases
were of two types. Most commonly the phrases had identical heads and the
relation of hyponymy existing between them was created through the
process of "syntagmatic modification" (Lyons 1977:309), a process
whereby the second unit of the apposition becomes a hyponym of the first
unit through the addition of a premodifier or postmodifier. In example 49,
the units contain the same head, *table*; the second unit is made more specific
and hence a hyponym of the first unit by the addition of a relative clause.
Likewise, in example 50, a postmodifier is added to the second unit to
specify the particular kind of tension mentioned in the first unit.

> (49) What I think we need, you see, is rooms with *a table, a
> table which students can sit round.* There's no sense in a seminar
> where someone is sitting at one end of the room and all the
> students are looking down towards the, the person who's sort of
> chairing it. (LLC s.3.4 47–57)

> (50) There had been *tension* in the plane during the silent
> descent, *a tension similar to the one now.* (Brown L19 330–40)

Less frequently the noun phrases in hyponymous appositions had different
heads. In both examples 51 and 52, different noun phrases in the second
unit specify, respectively, the types of social resources mentioned in the first
unit in example 51 and the types of wet-land crops mentioned in the first
unit in example 52.

> (51) In addition, in many cases, *a variety of concrete social
> resources – homemaker, day care, medical and financial aid –* must
> be reasonably available for the reality support needed to bolster

the family in its individual and collective coping and integrative efforts. (Brown J24 960–1010)

(52) It [the agricultural revolution] involved the transition from a pre-industrial agrarian society dependent on dry-land crops grown for subsistence, to a society where farmers have become increasingly innovative in technology and capitalist in mode of production, with *wet-land crops* (*sugar cane and rices*) as their main source of livelihood. (SEU w.9.6.43)

Although all form classes can be hyponyms (Lyons 1977:294), it was very uncommon in the corpora, as Table 3.8 demonstrates, for hyponymous appositions to consist of units that were not noun phrases. In non-nominal hyponymous appositions, as in nominal hyponymous appositions, there is a relation of meaning inclusion between the units in apposition. In example 53, the second unit of the apposition (*so peaceful and quiet*) makes more explicit just what is meant by *nice* in the first unit.

(53) It was *nice* then, *so peaceful and quiet*. (Brown N02 690)

Likewise, in example 54, the second unit (*half again as long as those of Beowulf*) specifies precisely the length of lines repeated more than once in the *Iliad* and the *Odyssey*, a length that is characterized very generally in the first unit as only *so long*.

(54) Thus one line in five from the *Iliad* and the *Odyssey* is to be found somewhere else in the two poems. The ratio is thoroughly remarkable, because the lines are *so long – half again as long as those of Beowulf*. (Brown J67 1700–40)

3.2 The semantic classes of apposition

Discussing the semantic relations existing between units in apposition is one way of characterizing their semantic structure. Another way to describe the semantics of apposition is to posit semantic classes of apposition, classes which depict the manner in which the second unit of an apposition provides information about the first unit that is more specific, less specific, or equally specific.

Table 3.9 lists the semantic classes into which appositions can be classified and the frequency with which these classes occurred in the corpora. As this table indicates, apposition is predominantly a relation in which the second unit of the apposition adds specificity to the interpretation of the first unit: the majority of appositions in the corpora (59 percent) consisted of constructions whose second unit contained information that was more specific than the first unit; the remaining appositions contained second units that were either less specific than the first units (16 percent) or equally as specific as them (25 percent).

Table 3.9. *The semantic classes of apposition*

Semantic class	Brown	LLC	SEU	Total
More specific				
Identification	323	239	451	1,013
Appellation	212	21	124	357
Particularization	49	49	40	138
Exemplification	42	80	55	177
Total	626	389	670	1,685 (59%)
Less specific				
Characterization	208	37	205	450 (16%)
Equally specific				
Paraphrase	165	258	143	566
Reorientation	26	32	13	71
Self-correction	1	62	6	69
Total	192	352	162	706 (25%)
Total	1,026	778	1,037	2,841 (100%)

Many of the semantic classes in Table 3.9 are taken from Quirk *et al.*'s (1985:1308–16) discussion of apposition. However, because Quirk *et al.*'s classes could not accurately account for all of the appositions in the corpora, two adjustments had to be made: in some instances, existing classes in Quirk *et al.* were redefined; in other instances, additional semantic classes had to be posited to account for semantic relationships between units that were not considered in Quirk *et al.*

3.2.1 *Semantic classes whose second units are more specific than their first units*

Four of the semantic classes in Table 3.9 specify ways that the second unit of an apposition can be more specific than the first unit. Nearly three-fourths of the appositions of this type fit into the semantic classes of identification and appellation; the remaining appositions were distributed much less frequently in the classes of particularization and exemplification.

3.2.1.1 *Identification*
In appositions within the class of identification, the first unit is a noun phrase with referring capabilities that is followed by a noun phrase, clause, or sentence that "identifies" the referent of the first unit. Either the two units will be coreferential (3.1.1.1), or the first unit will refer cataphorically to the second unit (3.1.1.3). If the apposition is a nonrestrictive apposition, the markers of apposition *namely* or *that is (to say)* can be optionally inserted

to indicate that the second unit identifies the first unit. If the apposition is a restrictive apposition, a marker is usually not permitted, except in instances where the obligatory marker *of* is required (2.1.3.2).

Because identification is such a common semantic class, a wide variety of appositions can be classified in it. Examples 55 and 56 contain units that are both noun phrases. In example 55, the second unit identifies the features of communism referred to in the first unit. In example 56, the second unit identifies the temperatures mentioned in the first unit.

> (55) Consider *the features of Utopian communism*: [namely] *generous public provision of the infirm*; *democratic and secret elections of all officers including priests*; *meals taken publicly in common refectories*; *a common habit or uniform prescribed for all citizens*; *even houses changed once a decade*...(Brown J57 1640–80)

> (56) Investigation of the high-temperature form, Phase I, is more difficult, particularly because at *the temperatures of measurement*, namely *150 °C. and 200 °C.*, the severe loss of intensity at the higher angles, occasioned by the increased thermal vibrations, limits the amount and precision of the neutron diffraction data. (SEU w.9.8.180–1, 181–1)

In examples 57 and 58, clauses follow an initial noun phrase. In example 57, the *that*-clause in the second unit identifies the referent of the pronoun *what* in the first unit and specifies precisely what writers on metaphor have pointed out. In example 58, the second unit identifies the administrative achievement mentioned in the first unit.

> (57) Most important of all, this description of the linguistic configuration of metaphor brings out the truth of *what* some writers on metaphor have been at pains to point out: that is, *that with a metaphor one can make a complex statement without complicating the grammatical construction of the sentence that carries the statement.* (SEU w.9.4.56–2, 56–3)

> (58) I was talking about *the administrative achievement* of *building up the supporting services for this great citizen army.* (LLC s.2.3 220–2)

In examples 59 and 60, sentences follow a noun phrase in the first unit. In example 59, the second unit identifies the two things mentioned in the first unit as having been said. In example 60, the second unit identifies the scoop referred to in the first unit.

> (59) Well, he says *two things*: *A, he's quite prepared to take a drop and then B, at the end, PS, what are you going to offer me?* (LLC s.2.6 636–41)

> (60) The Living Room has *another scoop: Jane Russell will make
> one of her rare night club singing appearances there, opening Jan. 22.*
> (Brown A16 1170–90)

3.2.1.2 *Appellation*

The semantic class of appellation is similar to the semantic class of
identification, except that in appositions within the class of appellation the
second unit "names" rather than identifies the first unit. Appositions
within the class of appellation consist of two noun phrases the second of
which is a proper noun. The noun phrases will be either coreferential
(3.1.1.1) or related by the relation of attribution (3.1.2.2). If the apposition
is a nonrestrictive apposition, the markers *namely* or *that is (to say)* can be
used to link the two units.

In example 61, the second unit names the individual referred to in the
first unit.

> (61) From its eight square windows the house watched them
> go; saw *one of them* – [that is to say] *Dinah* – stop at the
> wrought-iron gate in the low brick wall and look back hard at
> it. (SEU w.16.1.16)

In example 62, the second unit names the person whom the first unit
attributes as having the role of Secretary of Labor.

> (62) *Secretary of Labor Arthur Goldberg* will speak Sunday
> night at the Masonic Temple at a $25-a-plate dinner honoring
> Sen. Wayne L. Morse, D-Ore. (Brown A10 940–50)

And in example 63, the second unit names the book of Golding's referred
to in the first unit.

> (63) There's *another one [of Golding's books] I have read* too,
> [namely] *Pincher Martin.* (LLC s.3.1 296–7)

As Table 3.9 demonstrates, appositions within the class of appellation
tended to occur most frequently in the written samples of the corpora and
only rarely in the spoken samples. This distribution is a result of the fact
that the act of "naming" in the second unit of the apposition is an
important communicative act in writing, particularly in journalistic writing,
where naming the individuals one is reporting on is of prime importance
(4.4.2.3).

3.2.1.3 *Particularization*

In appositions within the class of particularization, the second unit of the
apposition "focuses" either the reference or meaning of the first unit.
Appositions within this class are of two types. They can be appositions
containing obligatory markers of apposition such as *particularly, especially,*

or *including* that have the ability of focusing one of the referents of the first unit (2.1.3.1). Alternatively, they can be appositions whose units are hyponyms (3.1.2.3), appositions in which the more specific second unit of the apposition contains a word whose meaning would be included within the meaning of the more general first unit.

In example 64, the second unit of the apposition focuses one particular group of people who are members of the class of poor individuals mentioned in the first unit.

> (64) As the rich got richer, *many of the poor* became poorer, especially *the members of low castes or 'outcastes' like the Untouchables who had never had much land in the first place.* (SEU w.9.6.47)

In example 65, the second unit singles out one woman who is a member of the class of women mentioned in the first unit.

> (65) He had known *women* like that, *one woman* in particular. (Brown N05 1020)

And in example 66, the second unit focuses on the type of grant referred to in the first unit that the individual wishes to receive.

> (66) I hope I would get *a grant, a major county award.* (LLC s.3.1 1058–60)

3.2.1.4 *Exemplification*

Appositions within the class of exemplification are like those within the class of particularization, except that in the class of exemplification the second unit provides an "example" of the first unit. Appositions within this class contain units that are in a part/whole relation to one another (3.1.1.2) and that are joined by the obligatory markers of apposition *such as, like,* or *for example* (2.1.3.1), markers that explicitly indicate that the second unit is an example of the first unit.

In example 67, the second unit gives an example of one of the diseases mentioned in the first unit.

> (67) A general physician, well, uses drugs. I mean that's his main, you know, he doesn't cut. He uses drugs and he'll treat, he'll treat *diseases* such as initially *a duodenal ulcer.* (LLC s.2.9 650–5)

In example 68, the second unit gives an example of a town that is close to Dogtown.

> (68) Today Dogtown is the only deserted village in all New England that I know of. There it sits, a small highland, with *towns* like *Gloucester* near by. (Brown L22 400–20)

And in example 69, the second unit provides examples of the agricultural outlays that have to be accounted for.

> (69) The farmer's net annual income after *all outlays in agriculture* have been accounted for (e.g. *wages, fertiliser costs, bullock hire, land taxi*), and after he has bought his household's food supply, amounts to 1,080 rupees, or the equivalent of 7.5 MJ per person per day. (SEU w.9.6.67)

3.2.2. *Semantic classes whose second units are less specific than their first units*

Only one semantic class – characterization – contains a second unit that is less specific than the first unit. Overall, as Table 3.9 illustrates, the class of characterization was a fairly frequently occurring semantic class in the corpora: while it occurred less frequently than the classes of identification and paraphrase, it occurred more frequently than the classes of appellation, particularization, exemplification, reorientation, and self-correction.

3.2.2.1 *Characterization*

Appositions within the class of characterization consist of a second unit that is a noun phrase that provides general "characteristics" of the first unit. The units of this kind of apposition are either coreferential (3.1.1.1) or attributive (3.1.2.2). If the units are coreferential, they will admit the marker of apposition *that is (to say)* or a relative pronoun followed by a form of the verb *be*; if the units are attributively related, they will not admit a marker of apposition but only a relative pronoun followed by a form of the verb *be*.

Examples 70 and 71 contain units that are coreferential and that therefore admit either a marker of apposition or a relative pronoun followed by a form of the verb *be*. In example 70, the individual named in the first unit is characterized as being someone from overseas. In example 71, the Republicans referred to in the first unit are characterized as being the third party in a particular political coalition.

> (70a) *David Prendergast*, [that is to say] *the man from overseas* – Prendergast, he's been in Southern Rhodesia. (LLC s.1.2 729–32)
> (70b) David Prendergast, [who is] the man from overseas...

> (71a) *The Republicans*, [that is to say] *the third party in the Centre-Left coalition*, would not come in to a new Government unless assured of complete Socialist support. (SEU w.12.1.16)
> (71b) The Republicans, [who are] the third party...

In examples 72 and 73, the units are not coreferential and therefore can only be joined by a relative clause followed by a form of the verb *be*. In example

72, the councillor named in the first unit is characterized as a Conservative in the second unit. In example 73, the individual named in the first unit is characterized as being a particular kind of secretary of state.

> (72) In May, shortly before the municipal elections, Councillor *Donald Finney*, [who is] *a Conservative*, alleged that Spon Lane was a centre of vice. (SEU w.12.1–6)

> (73) Helping foreign countries to build a sound political structure is more important than aiding them economically, *E.M. Martin*, [who is] *assistant secretary of state for economic affairs*[,] told members of the World Affairs Council Monday night. (Brown A10 090–120)

Most of the instances of appositions within the class of characterization occurred, as Table 3.9 points out, in the written samples of the corpora; fewer instances (8 percent) occurred in the spoken samples. This distribution is a result of the fact that providing characteristics about the first unit of an apposition is a communicative act most necessary in written English, particularly in journalistic English, a genre in which readers need to know particular characteristics of individuals reported in news stories (4.4.2.3).

3.2.3 *Semantic classes whose second units are equally as specific as their first units*

There are three semantic classes of appositions containing a second unit that is equally as specific as the first unit: the classes of paraphrase, reorientation, and self-correction. Two of these classes – reorientation and self-correction – were rather rare (see Table 3.9): each accounted for only 2 percent of the appositions in the corpora. On the other hand, the other class – paraphrase – occurred much more commonly, accounting for 20 percent of the appositions in the corpora.

3.2.3.1 *Paraphrase*
Appositions within the class of paraphrase consist of a second unit that "paraphrases" the meaning of the first unit. Appositions within this class consist of units that are phrases, clauses, or sentences related by the relation of synonymy (3.1.2.1). The units can be joined by two optional markers of apposition – *that is (to say)* and *in other words* – or the obligatory marker of apposition *or* (2.1.3.3).[6]

In example 74, the second unit of the apposition paraphrases the first unit and as a result provides a definition of what the writer means in the first unit by resemblance.

> (74) For this reason I would suggest that my reader should enter into an agreement with me that we shall speak, when we

> want to refer *to resemblance* (i.e. *to what makes the connection plausible*), of 'the link' between the two members of a metaphorical relationship. (SEU w.9.54-1)

In example 85, the second unit paraphrases the first unit and makes clear the meaning the speaker intended the phrase *imaginative works* to have.

> (75) Good guidebooks really are full of impressions, aren't they, whereas *imaginative works*, or *works of fiction*, often do blend facts in a distorted form. (LLC s.3.6 857-62)

And in example 76, the second unit is an entire sentence that paraphrases the meaning of the first sentence.

> (76) There is one man whose job is communication in the physical sense. That is, he looks after communication systems. (LLC s.2.2 1179-80)

As Table 3.9 indicates, appositions within the class of paraphrase were quite common in the spoken samples of the corpora and somewhat less common in the written samples. This distribution existed because it was quite common in the spoken samples for both units of an apposition to contain synonymous sentences in apposition with one another (2.1.4.2), a reflection of the spontaneous, unplanned nature of speech and the communicative need therefore to provide paraphrases (i.e. clarifications) of the sentences one utters (4.4.2.2).

3.2.3.2 *Reorientation*

Nominal appositions within the class of paraphrase, as the previous section demonstrated, contain a second unit that paraphrases the meaning of the first unit and therefore provides a different way of viewing the meaning of the first unit. Appositions within the class of reorientation serve a similar purpose. However, because units in the class of reorientation are coreferential (3.1.1.1), the second unit does not paraphrase the meaning of the first unit but instead refocuses its reference, providing a different way of viewing the first unit. The units in this type of apposition are definite noun phrases that can be joined optionally by the marker of apposition *that is (to say)*.

In example 77, the second unit of the apposition refocuses the reference of the first unit, suggesting that what the speaker will talk about is not necessarily the features of the book but rather its approach.

> (77) *The individual features*, [that is to say] *the individual attack* [*of the book*], is really through a kind of aesthetics of Piggott which is pretty much stolen straight from the thesis. (LLC s.3.6 478-83)

In example 78, the second unit alters the reader's perspective on the first unit, indicating that the woman referred to in the first unit is the wife of a particular individual.

> (78) WITH loud huzzahs for the artistic success of the Presbyterian-St. Luke's Fashion show still ringing in her ears, its director, *Helen Tieken Geraghty* ([that is to say] *Mrs. Maurice P. Geraghty*) is taking off tomorrow on a 56 day world trip which should earn her even greater acclaim as director of entertainment of next summer's International Trade fair. (Brown A16 510–60)

And in example 79, the second unit of the apposition shifts the focus of the reference of the first unit, suggesting that the academic world is not simply the stronghold of values but the center of these values.

> (79) The world was a cheap commercial project, run by profiteers, which disseminated bad taste, poor values, shoddy goods and cowboy films on television among a society held up to permanent ransom by these active rogues. Against this in his vision he was inclined to set the academic world, which seemed to him, though decreasingly so, *the one stronghold of values*, [that is to say] *the one centre from which the world was resisted*. (SEU w.16.2.106–2)

3.2.3.3 *Self-correction*

In appositions within the class of self-correction, the second unit "corrects" a mistake made in the first unit. The units in appositions of this type are noun phrases exhibiting speaker coreference (3.1.1.1) and can be optionally joined by the markers of apposition *or* or *or rather*. Because appositions of this type are self-correcting in nature, they tended to occur most frequently, as Table 3.9 indicated, in the spoken samples (4.4.2.1), which consisted exclusively of spontaneous conversations, and only very rarely in the written samples, which represented edited writing.

Examples 80–83 contain appositions within the class of self-correction. In each of these appositions, the second unit corrects a mistake of meaning or reference made in the first unit. In examples 80 and 81, the second units correct errors of meaning made in the first units. In example 80, the second unit, *transcriptions*, is a word whose meaning is more accurate than the meaning of the first unit, *transcripts*.

> (80) I think they, they, they have *transcripts*, [or] *transcriptions* shall I say, not transcripts. Transcripts are what the Bishop has. (LLC s.1.9 376–9)

In example 81, the second unit, *my great uncle Arthur*, more accurately expresses the speaker's relationship to the uncle than does the first unit, *my uncle Arthur*.

> (81) I keep thinking of *my uncle Arthur*, or rather *my great uncle Arthur*, who... (LLC s.1.106–8)

In examples 82 and 83, the second units contain noun phrases that correct errors in reference rather than meaning made in the first units of the appositions. In example 82, the second unit contains a pronoun that precisely corrects an error in pronoun reference made in the first unit.

> (82) "I wondered if you would put *my* – [or] *our* – names in it [the book]. And yours." (SEU w.16.5.25–4)

In example 83, on the other hand, the speaker cannot precisely correct the reference of the first unit because he does not know precisely who the correct referent is. Therefore, in the second unit he uses an indefinite noun phrase to correct the first unit and to indicate to the best of his knowledge who the correct referent is.

> (83) He entertained *Colonel House* or *whoever the American representative was*. (LLC s.2.3 564–5)

3.3 Restrictive and nonrestrictive apposition

In addition to being related by various semantic relations and falling into various semantic classes, units in apposition can be characterized by whether or not the second unit of the apposition restricts the reference of the first unit.

The majority of the 2,841 appositions in the corpora (1,543, or 54 percent) were either nominal appositions that were always nonrestrictive or non-nominal appositions for which the notions restrictive and nonrestrictive were not relevant. These appositions will not be discussed in this section, since the restrictive/nonrestrictive dichotomy does not apply to them. Instead, the focus of this section will be the remaining appositions in the corpora for which the restrictive/nonrestrictive distinction was relevant. Of the 1,298 appositions falling into this category, 813 (or 63 percent) were restrictive and 485 (or 37 percent) were nonrestrictive. This distribution roughly parallels the distribution of restrictive and nonrestrictive relative clauses that Taglicht (1977:76) found in the written samples of the London Corpus that he studied: of the 97 relative clauses Taglicht isolated in his corpus, 56 (or 57 percent) were restrictive and 41 (or 43 percent) were nonrestrictive.

Whether an apposition receives a restrictive or a nonrestrictive interpretation depends crucially on the syntactic form of the apposition and on whether the first unit of the apposition is a noun phrase capable of taking a restrictive or nonrestrictive second unit. Example 85, for instance, is a restrictive apposition because it has a syntactic form that permits restrictive apposition – the first unit is a definite noun phrase, the second unit a

Table 3.10. *Nominal appositions with restrictive/nonrestrictive interpretations*

Form	R	NR	Total
NP (d) + citations, measurements, titles, etc.	155 (68%)	74 (32%)	229
NP (−det) + proper NP	129 (100%)	0 (0%)	129
NP (d) + proper NP	34 (20%)	133 (80%)	167
NP (d) + NP (d)	2 (1%)	136 (99%)	138
Proper NP + NP (d)	7 (7%)	87 (93%)	94
Total	327 (43%)	430 (57%)	757

−det = NP lacking determiner
d = definite

linguistic citation – and because the first unit is a cataphoric-linked nominal (Lucas 1974: 100), a nominal whose determiner points ahead to a unit that restricts the reference of the nominal.

> (84) In order for the definitions to yield the desired results, we have to interpret *the words 'stand for' and 'about'* in the light of our knowledge of what is being defined. (SEU w.9.1.145–3)

In the remainder of this section, the constraints on restrictive and nonrestrictive apposition will be discussed as they apply to the three kinds of constructions that are capable of being restrictive and/or nonrestrictive: certain kinds of nominal appositions, appositions whose second units are clauses, and appositions whose units are joined by the obligatory markers of apposition *such as*, *like*, and *of*.

3.3.1 *Restrictive and nonrestrictive nominal appositions*

Table 3.10 outlines the nominal appositions in the corpora that were either always restrictive or both restrictive and nonrestrictive. As this table indicates, these appositions ranged from being always restrictive to rarely restrictive.

3.3.1.1 *Restrictive appositions containing units lacking determiners*
Appositions were always restrictive if they contained a second unit that was a proper noun and a first unit that was a noun phrase lacking a determiner:

> (85) "Emory University's charter and by-laws have never required admission or rejection of students on the basis of race," *board chairman Henry L. Bowden* stated. (Brown A22 30–50)

This kind of apposition is classified as restrictive primarily because the two units of the apposition are not separated by comma intonation. However, the tonal integration existing between the units is largely the result of these appositions being on a gradient between titles and appositions (2.5.4.1). Moreover, appositions of this type differ from other restrictive appositions in one key respect: because the first units of such appositions contain a noun phrase lacking a determiner, the noun phrase has no referring value and therefore cannot have its reference restricted. Because of this characteristic, appositions such as those in example 85 must be considered quasi-restrictive appositions at best.

3.3.1.2 *Restrictive and nonrestrictive appositions containing citations, measurements, and titles*

Examples 86 and 87 contain appositions whose first units were definite and whose second units were citations, measurements, titles, etc. Such appositions were predominantly restrictive, as Table 3.10 demonstrates, because their first units most frequently contained a cataphoric-linked nominal, a noun phrase pointing ahead to the second unit and restricting its reference.

> (86) Otherwise I shall end up like *the song* " *The Seven Drunken Knights.*" (LLC s.2.11 830–1)

This kind of apposition was infrequently nonrestrictive because it was less likely for their first units to contain an anaphoric-linked nominal (Lucas 1974:100), a noun phrase containing a determiner that ties the interpretation of the noun phrase to the context in which it occurs. In example 87, presumably it is clear from the context just what the Prime Minister's favourite expression is. Consequently, the second unit does not restrict the reference of the first unit but simply adds extra information about it.

> (87) Last night some of the gloomier M.P.'s were predicting that *The Prime Minster's favourite chestnut,* "*June – pause – or October,*" may now be revised to "October – pause – or September – pause – or November." (SEU w.12.2.2)

3.3.1.3 *Restrictive and nonrestrictive appositions containing definite noun phrases in both units*

Examples 88 and 89 illustrate restrictive and nonrestrictive instances of appositions whose first unit was a definite noun phrase and whose second unit was a proper noun. Example 88 is a restrictive apposition because the first unit, *this woman*, is quite general and, additionally, a cataphoric-linked nominal; its reference is restricted by the very specific second unit, *Bandra*, that follows it.

> (88) Do you think we could remove *this woman Bandra* on grounds of age? (LLC s.2.6 1143)

Example 89, on the other hand, contains a nonrestrictive apposition because the first unit is very specific and contains an anaphoric-linked nominal that does not restrict the reference of the first unit but merely names the father referred to in the first unit.

> (89) Because of the recent death of *the bride's father, Frederick B. Hamm*, the marriage of Miss Terry Hamm to John Bruce Parichy will be a small one at noon tomorrow in St. Bernadine's church, Forest Park. (Brown A16 330–50)

Examples 90 and 91 contain restrictive and nonrestrictive instances of appositions whose units were both definite noun phrases. As Table 3.10 illustrates, restrictive appositions of this type were quite rare and were restricted in the corpora to stereotypical constructions such as 90:

> (90) CAMDEN's colourful Greater London councillor Charlie Rossi boycotted the ceremony and razzmatazz on the Thames on Tuesday as *Her Majesty the Queen* formally opened the new multi-million pound flood barrier. (SEU w.12.7e2)

It was most common for appositions of this type to be nonrestrictive and to contain a first unit that was an anaphoric-linked nominal:

> (91) *The first twenty thousand pounds, the original grant*, is committed, you see, but I thought it was never allowed to be spread, spread, over three years. (LLC s.1.2 782–6)

Examples 92 and 93 contain instances of restrictive and nonrestrictive appositions whose first units were proper nouns and whose second units were definite noun phrases. Restrictive instances of this kind of apposition were rare in the corpora, largely because the first unit of such appositions is a proper noun, a nominal whose reference is unique and therefore difficult to restrict. Restrictive instances of such appositions are possible only if the second unit restricts some characteristic of the first unit. In example 92, the second unit of the apposition, *the man*, serves to emphasize that the speaker of the sentence is stressing a characteristic of Eisenhower as an individual rather than as, say, a former president of the United States.

> (92) Sunday he [Richard J. Hughes] added, "We can love *Eisenhower the man*, even if we considered him a mediocre president, but there is nothing left of the Republican Party without his leadership." (Brown A06 170–200)

Except for rare instances such as the apposition in example 92, it was most common for appositions having this form to be nonrestrictive:

> (93) *Mr. Frederick Manning, the man who piloted Sir Gerald Nabarro, Tory M.P. for Kidderminster, through four successful election campaigns*, died at the wheel of his car yesterday. (SEU w.12.2.15)

Table 3.11. *Nominal/clausal appositions with restrictive and nonrestrictive interpretations*

Form	R	NR	Total
NP (d) + *that*-clause	170 (95%)	9 (5%)	179
NP (i) + *that*-clause	33 (89%)	4 (11%)	37
NP (i) + *to*-clause	20 (83%)	4 (17%)	24
NP (d) + *to*-clause	26	0	26
NP (d) + clause	3	6	9
NP (i) + clause	0	4	4
Total	252 (90%)	27 (10%)	279

d = definite
i = indefinite

3.3.2 *Restrictive and nonrestrictive appositions whose second units are clauses*

Table 3.11 lists the restrictive and nonrestrictive appositions in the corpora whose first units were definite or indefinite noun phrases and whose second units were clauses. Such appositions, as this table indicates, were overwhelmingly restrictive because their first units were predominantly cataphoric-linked nominals. In example 94, the determiner *the* before *simple reason* points ahead to the *that*-clause which follows it; this clause, in turn, restricts the reference of the noun phrase, indicating precisely just which reason is being referred to in the sentence.

> (94) I mean, I know that Americans have a wonderful standard of living for some things, but frankly, our standard of living has never been as high as it was when, when I was young, for *the simple reason that two inside servants and one outside full-time is equivalent to a hell of a lot of other things.* (LLC s.1.13 499–508)

In example 95, the determiner *his* before *desire* likewise points ahead to the *to*-clause which it precedes, a clause which restricts the reference of the noun phrase and indicates the particular desire being referred to.

> (95) The first speaker was Amos C. Barstow who had been unanimously chosen president of the meeting. He spoke of *his desire to promote the abolition of slavery by peaceable means* and he compared John Brown of Harper's Ferry to the John Brown of Rhode Island's colonial period. (Brown j58 1420–60)

Although nonrestrictive appositions of this type are possible, they occurred only sporadically in the corpora primarily for pragmatic reasons. Because these kinds of appositions fit into the semantic class of identification (3.2.1.1), they contain a second unit that identifies the referent of the first unit. In order for these appositions to be nonrestrictive, they will have to contain a first unit that is an anaphoric-linked nominal. And if the first unit is this kind of nominal, the referent of the nominal will be clear from the context and there will therefore be little need to identify its referent by adding a second unit. For instance, in example 96a, *decision* is a noun phrase capable of being followed by a second unit that is a *to*-clause (example 96b). However, since the referent of this noun phrase is clear from the context, adding a second unit results in a highly redundant and unacceptable sentence.

> (96a) The three leaders of Laos agreed today to begin negotiations tomorrow on forming a coalition government that would unite the war-ridden kingdom. *The decision* was made in Zurich by Prince Boun Qum, Premier of the pro-Western royal Government...(Brown A07 1720–50)
>
> (96b) ?The three leaders of Laos agreed today to begin negotiations tomorrow on forming a coalition government that would unite the war-ridden kingdom. *The decision [to begin negotiations tomorrow on forming a coalition government that would unite the war-ridden kingdom]* was made in Zurich...

Nonrestrictive instances of these appositions will occur only if there is some need to reintroduce into the discourse the referent of the first unit. In example 97, Eliot's views on Shakespeare are discussed early on in the discourse. When they are reintroduced later, the speaker identifies them in the second unit of a nonrestrictive apposition simply to remind the person he is speaking with just what the views discussed earlier were.

> (97) A: I've read some of – not particularly known as a Shakespearean critic, Eliot, his more general essays on Shakespeare.
>
> B: Do you know his remarks on *Hamlet*?
>
> A: Yes, I have read them, sir.
>
> B: What are they? Will you give me the gist of his approach?
>
> A: He, he believes that, that Shakespeare attempts in *Hamlet* something which he, he didn't understand himself even, and to that, to that there, that's why it raises so many problems of interpretation...[16 tone units later]
>
> B: Now, let's go back to *Hamlet* then. Do you agree with *Eliot's view, that this is an imperfect play*? (LLC s.3.5 969–1005)

Table 3.12. *Appositions containing obligatory markers of apposition with restrictive and nonrestrictive interpretations*

Form	R	NR	Total
NP (i) + *such as* + NP	141 (83%)	28 (17%)	169
like			
NP (d) + *of* + NP	54	0	54
clause	39	0	39
Total	234 (89%)	28 (11%)	262

d = definite
i = indefinite

3.3.3 *Restrictive and nonrestrictive appositions containing obligatory markers of apposition.*

Table 3.12 details the frequency of restrictive and nonrestrictive occurrences of appositions consisting of the obligatory markers of apposition *of*, *such as*, and *like*. As this table illustrates, these appositions were virtually always restrictive; they were nonrestrictive only if they contained the markers *such as* and *like*.

Appositions containing the marker *of* were always restrictive because they contained first units headed by cataphoric-linked nominals. In examples 98 and 99, the noun phrases in the first units point ahead to constituents in the second units that restrict the reference of the first units.

> (98) In the morning Harold announced *his intention* of *going to church*. (SEU w.16.5.24–4)

> (99) What did they think about *the vexed question* of *mixed colleges*? (LLC s.1.3 693–5)

Unlike appositions containing the marker *of*, those containing the markers *such as* or *like* could be either restrictive or nonrestrictive. Whether these appositions were restrictive or nonrestrictive depended upon whether the first unit was a categorical nominal or a partitive nominal (Lucas 1974:100).

If the first unit was a categorical nominal, it had generic reference and for semantic reasons could therefore occur only in a restrictive apposition. In example 100, the noun phrase in the first unit, *a man*, refers to a class of individuals including the individual *Garrett* mentioned in the second unit.

> (100) Hillard was appalled, he had not dreamed that this could happen and so quickly to *a man* like *Garrett*. (SEU w.16.8.62)

In example 101, the noun phrase in the first unit refers to a class of heavy pastes whose reference is restricted to the kinds of pastes referred to in the second unit.

> (101) Such an instrument is expected to be especially useful if it could be used to measure the elasticity of *heavy pastes* such as *printing inks, paints, adhesive, molten plastics, and bread dough*, for the elasticity is related to those various properties termed "length," "shortness," "spinnability," etc., which are usually judged by subjective methods at present. (Brown J03 590–660)

If the first unit was a partitive nominal, it had specific reference and could be either restrictive or nonrestrictive. Even though the restrictive/nonrestrictive dichotomy applies to appositions of this type, there is little difference in meaning between restrictive and nonrestrictive instances of these appositions. In example 102a, for instance, the first unit refers to an unknown group of plays; the second unit does not restrict the reference of the first unit but instead provides an example of one of the plays. There would be little change in meaning if the comma intonation was omitted.

> (102a) I could take perhaps the *Oresteia*, or do you think I should take *an early play*, like *the Prometheus*? (LLC s.1.4 1203–5)
> (102b) ...or do you think I should take *an early play* like *the Prometheus*?

The apposition in example 103a behaves in a similar manner. Because the second unit in example 103a is set off by a comma, it does not restrict the reference of the first unit but merely provides an example of one of the works referred to in the first unit. However, when the second unit is not set off by a comma (example 103b), it restricts the reference of the first unit to only referring to the book *The Sane Society* mentioned in the second unit.

> (103a) Despite its rather long intellectual history, alienation is still a promising hypothesis and not a verified theory. The idea has received much attention in philosophy, in literature, and in *a few works of general social criticism*, such as *The Sane Society*. (Brown J63 370–410)
> (103b) The idea has received much attention...*in a few works of general social criticism* such as *The Sane Society*.

3.4 The semantic gradient of apposition

In 2.5 it was demonstrated that certain appositions are syntactically more appositional than other appositions and that there therefore exists a syntactic gradient of apposition. Because apposition is such a semantically diverse relation, it is also possible to identify a semantic gradient of apposition: "a semantic scale running from equivalence (i.e. 'most

Fig. 3.1. The semantic gradient of apposition

Most appositional	Congruence relation of "identity"
	Coreference
	Synonymy
	Congruence relation of "semi-identity"
	Cataphoric reference
	Congruence relation of "inclusion"
	Attribution
	Hyponymy
Least appositional	Part/whole relations

Adapted from Quirk *et al.* (1985:1308)

appositive') to loose and unequal relationship ('least appositive')..."
(Quirk *et al.* 1985:1308). The semantic gradient of apposition can be best
illustrated if the semantic relationships existing between units in apposition
are classified according to the particular "congruence relations" in Cruse
(1986:86–7) that they satisfy. Although Cruse intended these relations to
capture the degree of similarity of meaning between two lexical items, they
can also be used to illustrate the semantic gradient of apposition.

Figure 3.1 details the semantic relations existing between units in
apposition according to the position on the semantic gradient into which
they can be placed. Highest on the semantic gradient are appositions whose
units are related by semantic relations satisfying Cruse's congruence
relation of identity: "class A and class B have the same members" (Cruse
1986:87). Satisfying this relation are appositions whose units are related by
the relations of coreference and synonymy, relations indicating identity of
reference (example 104) or identity of meaning (example 105):

> (104) Have you ever been to *it, the Biograph*? (LLC s.2.10
> 671–2)

> (105) In this puddled soil the exchange of air between
> atmosphere and soil is minimised, so creating an *anaerobic*
> (*oxygen-deficient*) [italics mine] environment for roots, the so-
> called *reduced zone* [italics in original]. (SEU w.9.6.16–17)

Intermediate on the gradient are appositions in which the first unit refers
cataphorically to the second unit. Because a referential relation exists
between the two units in this kind of apposition, this semantic relation is
somewhat similar to the relation of coreference. However, because the
second unit has no referring value, there does not exist true identity of
reference between the two units. Hence, these appositions are not
semantically as appositional as appositions whose units are coreferential:

> (106) This method in general solved *the problem* of *obtaining fairly equal concentrations of reactants in each of the six cells from a set.* (Brown J06 79–81)

At the same time, these appositions are more appositional than those that are lowest on the semantic gradient of apposition. Appositions at this level contain units that satisfy Cruse's congruence relation of inclusion: "class B is wholly included within class A" (Cruse 1986:87). Satisfying this relation are appositions whose units are related by the remaining semantic relations: attribution, hyponymy, and part/whole relations. In example 107, the units are related by the relation of attribution, a relation which indicates in this instance that the farm mentioned in the first unit, Port Howard, is of the class of farms having the characteristic of being owned by a particular British firm.

> (107) After a day's flying from farm to farm in West Falkland yesterday, Lord Chalfont told the people of *Port Howard*, *a large sheep farm owned by the British firm of Waldrons*, that he had seen enough indications to know how the people think. (SEU w.12.4.29)

In example 108, the units are related by the relation of hyponymy. In this example, the meaning of the second unit, *a hell of a lot*, expresses a degree of knowledge that would be a subset of the knowledge expressed by the first unit, *a lot*.

> (108) I mean, this, the chap that got it, I mean, has worked consistently all the way through the course, you know, almost every night, and he knows *a lot, a hell of a lot.* (LLC s.2.9 408–16)

And in example 109, a part/whole relation exists between the two units: the reference of the second unit would be included within the reference of the first unit.

> (109) When we look at *countries* like *Iran, Iraq, Pakistan, and Burma*, where substantial progress has been made in creating a minimum supply of modern men and of social overhead capital, and where institutions of centralized government exist, we find a second category of countries with a different set of problems and hence different priorities for policy. (Brown J22 36–41)

4   The pragmatics of apposition

The two previous chapters detailed, respectively, the syntactic and semantic characteristics of units in apposition. In this chapter, the emphasis will be the pragmatic characteristics of apposition.

Thematically, apposition is a relation in which the second unit of the apposition either wholly or partially provides new information about the first unit (4.1), new information that can be optionally introduced by a marker of apposition (4.2). Because appositions have this thematic characteristic, they are better suited to some contexts than to others and were therefore distributed differently across the genres of the corpora. In general, appositions occurred most frequently in those genres (such as press reportage) in which there was a communicative need for new information to be provided about the first unit of the apposition (4.3). In addition, certain types of appositions occurred more frequently in some genres than in others (4.4) because certain kinds of appositions (e.g. those within the semantic class of paraphrase) are communicatively more necessary in some genres (e.g. spontaneous conversation) than in others (e.g. fiction).

4.1 The thematic characteristics of units in apposition

Semantically, apposition is a relation whose units are related by various kinds of equivalence (3.4): referentially, for instance, the two units of an apposition can exhibit exact equivalence (coreference) or partial equivalence (part/whole relations). Thematically, however, the units of an apposition are characterized by various degrees of non-equivalence: the second unit of an apposition is not equivalent to the first unit but rather either wholly or partially provides new information about the first unit.[1] Apposition is therefore an "additive" relation (Halliday and Hasan 1976:244f), a relation in which the second unit of the apposition "adds" to the flow of discourse.

Examples 1 and 2 illustrate the additive function of units in apposition. In example 1, the second unit of the apposition provides entirely new information about the first unit because the second unit, *the pericardium*, contains information not previously introduced into the discourse in which this sentence occurs.

Table 4.1. *Appositions in the individual corpora containing new and old information*

Information	Brown	LLC	SEU	Total
Old	100 (10%)	227 (29%)	74 (7%)	401 (14%)
New	926 (90%)	551 (71%)	963 (93%)	2,440 (86%)
Total	1,026 (100%)	778 (100%)	1,037 (100%)	2,841 (100%)

(1) The heart is suspended in *a special portion of the coelom, the pericardium*, whose walls are supported by cartilage. (SEU W.9.7.91–1)

In contrast, in example 2, only part of the second unit of the apposition provides new information about the first unit: while the end of the second unit contains new information (*from above*), the beginning of the unit repeats information (*a visitor*) introduced into the discourse in the first unit of the apposition.

(2) My agreement carries me from one division to another but only in the capacity as a, of *a visitor, a visitor from above*, you see. (LLC S.2.2 1241–4)

The vast majority of appositions in the corpora (86 percent), as Table 4.1 illustrates, contained second units consisting entirely of new information; relatively few appositions (14 percent) were comprised of second units consisting only partially of new information. There were two considerations that affected the placement of information in the second unit of an apposition. First of all, in those appositions whose second units contained both old and new information, the information was organized along the principles of communicative dynamism (cf. Firbas 1980 and 1986). Secondly, the inclusion of old information in the second units of appositions was not arbitrary but was motivated by specific communicative factors.

4.1.1 *The distribution of old and new information in the second units of appositions*

Table 4.2 lists the three syntactic forms whose second units contained old information. In each of these appositions, the principle of communicative dynamism guided the ordering of new and old information. That is to say, in the second units of each of these appositions, unless other factors intervened, the old information occurred at the beginning of the unit and the new information at the end.

In examples 3 and 4, the ordering of information in the second units strictly followed the principles of communicative dynamism: there is a

Table 4.2. *The syntactic forms of appositions containing old information in the second unit*

Form	Brown	LLC	SEU	Total
Clause				
Sentence	35	115	17	167
Subor clause	17	16	19	52
Predication	5	9	2	16
Total	57	140	38	235 (59%)
NP	35	70	23	128 (32%)
Prep phrase	8	17	13	38 (9%)
Total	100	227	74	401 (100%)

strict "linear progression" in each of these examples "from low to high information value" (Quirk *et al.* 1985:1356–7). In example 3, the old information (*he owns*), which has low information value, is placed at the beginning of the second unit and is followed by the new information (*the difference between...*), which has higher information value.

> (3) He [a homeowner] owns everything that isn't, isn't given to the mortgage company. [That is to say] he owns the difference between what is bespoke and its actual value. (LLC s.2.2 515–17)

A similar pattern can be found in example 4, with the old information (*was*) beginning the second unit and the new information (*thinner*) ending it.

> (4) His face *was altered*, [that is to say] *was thinner*, the eyes puffed but the cheeks drawn in, his fingers moved all the time about the rim of his glass, or smoothed down the patch of thinning hair. (SEU w.16.8.61–2)

In some instances, however, it is not possible, as Firbas (1986:43–7) observes, to strictly follow the principle of communicative dynamism because other factors will more heavily influence the placement of information in a clause or phrase. In example 5, the old information (*place*) occurs towards the middle of the second unit because some of the new information (*a rather more welcoming*) is a determiner followed by a pre-modifier that for syntactic reasons can be placed only at the start of the second unit.

> (5) For the members of the unit it had been *just another place*; *a rather more welcoming place, in the circumstances, than the one they had left, but one that was physically not unlike it.* (SEU w.16.7.32–4)

In example 6, because the old information in the second unit (*my supporters*) is functioning as object of a preposition, syntactically it must be placed at the end of the second unit rather than at the beginning of it.

> (6) I felt before I went that they were seeing me *because of my supporters*, you know, *out of deference to my supporters*. (LLC s.1.3 1021–5)

4.1.2 *Communicative factors motivating the placement of old information in the second unit of an apposition*

There were three primary reasons why the second unit of an apposition contained old information: to aid in the comprehension and production of spoken texts, to create parallelism, and to emphasize important information in the apposition.

In addition to detailing the total number of appositions in the corpora containing old and new information, Table 4.1 lists the percentage of appositions in each of the corpora that contained old and new information. As this table shows, while nearly one-third of the appositions in the spoken corpus contained old information, only about a tenth of the appositions in the written corpora contained old information. Appositions containing old information in their second units were more likely to occur in the spoken corpus because the repetition achieved by repeating old information serves a specific communicative function in speech: as Tannen (1987:582) has noted, old information aids in the production of speech by allowing "a speaker to produce fluent speech while formulating what to say next"; it aids in the comprehension of speech by enabling "a hearer to receive information at roughly the rate the speaker is producing it."

Both of these communicative goals are achieved in the appositions in examples 7 and 8. In each of these examples, the repeated information allows the speaker time to think about what he or she plans to add as new information about the first unit. At the same time, the repetition keeps the old information in the hearer's short-term memory until the new information can be provided.

> (7) All of the three Exton graduates were girls who were *already involved in their research*, [that is to say] *already involved in their BPharm*. (LLC s.1.3 279–81)

> (8) We are not thinking of a scholarly production. [That is to say] we are not thinking of re-editing texts. (LLC s.3.2 1152–4)

While the old information in the examples above promotes communication in spoken texts, in other contexts the repetition of old information in the second unit serves a stylistic function. In examples 9a and 10a below, the prepositions are repeated to create parallel structures and avoid a stylistically awkward construction (9b and 10b).

> (9a) Geach here uses the phrases 'logical subject', 'logical predicate', as Frege uses 'proper name', 'predicative expression', to speak *of items of List II*, i.e. *of linguistic parts of a statement*. (SEU w.9.1 142–2, 143–1)
>
> (9b) ?... Frege uses 'proper name', 'predicative expression', to speak of items of List II, i.e. linguistic parts of a statement.

> (10a) I'm just explaining how I acquired a sewing-machine *by foul means*, [that is to say] *by writing an instruction booklet for one and saying I must have this if I'm going to write the booklet when I'd written the booklet and it was all over.* (LLC s.1.3 169–77)
>
> (10b) ?I'm just explaining how I acquired a sewing-machine by foul means, [that is to say] writing an instruction booklet for one and saying...

In examples 11 and 12, noun phrases are repeated in the second units for purposes of emphasis. Both of these examples contain instances of "resumptive modifiers," a noun phrase repeated at the beginning of the second unit to "highlight important words" (Williams 1981:850). In example 11, the noun phrase *the men* is repeated to emphasize the fact that it is ironic that the person mentioned at the beginning of the excerpt is being chased by individuals he knew well.

> (11) He knew who was riding after him – *the men he had known all his life, the men who had worked for him, sworn their loyalty to him.* (Brown n02 1540–50)

In example 12, the repetition of *a condition* emphasizes the seriousness of psychical blindness.

> (12) Psychical blindness is *a condition in which there is a total absence of visual memory-images, a condition in which, for example, one is unable to remember something just seen or to conjure up a memory-picture of the visible appearance of a well-known friend in his absence.* (Brown j52 60–100)

4.2   Optional markers of apposition

Table 4.3 lists the optional markers of apposition that occurred in the corpora and the frequency with which they occurred.[2] Optional markers of apposition, as this table demonstrates, were very uncommon: they introduced the second unit of an apposition in only 3 percent of the appositions in the corpora; most appositions (97 percent) contained either no marker or an obligatory marker.

Table 4.3. *Optional markers of apposition*

Marker	Brown	LLC	SEU	Total
None	1,006	758	1,005	2,769 (97%)
That is	11	8	10	29
That is to say	1	5	4	10
i.e.	2	1	6	9
e.g.	4	1	3	8
viz	0	0	5	5
Namely	1	0	3	4
In other words	1	3	0	4
Say	0	2	1	3
Total	1,026	778	1,037	2,841 (100%)

Optional markers of apposition serve the function of explicitly indicating whether the information in the second unit is "expository" or "exemplifying," the two main additive functions (4.1) that units in an apposition serve (Halliday and Hasan 1976:248–50). If the relation between the units is expository (i.e. if the units are referentially or semantically equivalent [cf. 3.1.1.1 and 3.1.2.1]), markers such as *that is (to say)*, *i.e.*, *namely*, *viz*, and *in other words* were used to introduce the second unit:

> (13) It was shown that correction for secondary extinction was only necessary for *intense reflections*, namely *(310) and (400)*, measured with the cO axis vertical. (SEU w.9.8 170–1)

> (14) And he [the patient] could recognize, by touch alone, articles which he had handled immediately before, even though they were altogether unfamiliar to him and could not be identified by him; that is, he was unaware what kind of objects they were or what their use was. (Brown J53 650–80)

If, on the other hand, the relation between the units was exemplifying (i.e. if the units were referentially and semantically only semi–equivalent [cf. 3.1.1.1 and 3.1.2.1]), markers such as *that is (to say)*, *i.e.*, *namely*, *viz*, and *in other words* were used to introduce the second unit:

> (15) The farmer's net annual income after *all outlays in agriculture* have been accounted for (e.g. *wages, fertiliser costs, bullock hire, land tax*), and after he has bought his household's food supply, amounts to 1,080 rupees, or the equivalent of 7.5 MJ per person per day. (SEU w.9.6.67)

> (16) Take *a good example*, say *lung cancer*. Now the symptoms the patient may complain of, many symptoms, he may feel

Table 4.4. *Optional markers of apposition in the genres of the corpora*

Genre	Number of markers
Learned, humanistic	26 (36%)
Learned, scientific	20 (28%)
Intimates/equals	6
Disparates	5
Equals	5
Intimates	4
Fiction	4
Press	2
Total	72

breathless, right. Now that symptom is not a symptom of lung cancer. (LLC s.2.9 1083–9)

So few optional markers of apposition occurred in the corpora that it is difficult to determine precisely why they were so infrequent. However, one reason might be that optional markers are stylistically marked. As Table 4.4 illustrates, nearly two-thirds (64 percent) of the optional markers occurred in the learned genres of the corpora, suggesting that optional markers are indicators of formal style and would therefore be inappropriate in less formal styles, such as spontaneous conversation, fiction, and press reportage.

4.3 The frequency of occurrence of appositions across the genres of the corpora

Table 4.5 details the frequency with which appositions occurred in the various genres of the corpora. As this table reveals, appositions were distributed quite unevenly across the genres of the corpora: the genres of fiction and conversation contained the fewest instances of appositions (5.6 and 6.5 appositions per thousand words, respectively), the genres of learned writing and press writing the most (9.4 and 10.8 appositions per thousand words, respectively).[3] This skewed distribution existed in the corpora because appositions are communicatively more necessary in some genres than in others. Specifically, appositions are most necessary in genres in which discourse participants possess a low amount of shared knowledge – in genres in which there is some need to add to the flow of discourse in the way that appositions do. In general, as Biber (1988:46) observes, spontaneous conversation takes place between individuals possessing a high amount of shared personal knowledge; written texts, in contrast, consist of discourse participants with a low amount of shared personal knowledge.

Table 4.5. *Appositions per genre*

Genre	Number of appositions	Appositions per 1,000 words
Fiction		
SEU	201	5.0
Brown	244	6.1
Total	445	5.6
Conversation		
Intimates	158	5.3
Equals	169	5.6
Disparates	223	7.4
Intimates/equals	228	7.6
Total	778	6.5
Learned		
Scientific (Brown)	132	6.6
Scientific (SEU)	197	9.9
Humanistic (Brown)	180	9.0
Humanistic (SEU)	245	12.3
Total	754	9.4
Press		
SEU	394	9.9
Brown	470	11.8
Total	864	10.8
Total	2,841	7.9

And this difference explains why two of the written genres – learned writing and press writing – had more appositions than the spoken genres.

But this general difference between speech and writing does not explain why the fictional genre, a written genre, had the fewest appositions, why the individual spoken genres contained variable numbers of appositions, and why the learned humanistic genre contained more appositions than the learned scientific genre. To explain the variable occurrence of appositions within these genres, we must examine the extent to which discourse participants within a given genre will vary in terms of the shared personal knowledge that they possess and explore other reasons giving rise to variation within a genre.

4.3.1 *Variation within the written genres*

Even though fiction is a written genre, it contained far fewer appositions than the two other written genres: learned writing and press writing (see Table 4.5). It is not surprising that the press and learned genres contained so many appositions: press writing, for instance, particularly press reportage, must appeal to a very wide and diverse audience; consequently, journalists must assume little shared knowledge with the audience they are writing for. It is somewhat surprising, however, that the fictional genre contained so few appositions, since one would expect authors writing in this genre to want to provide, for instance, descriptive information about characters, a communicative task well suited to appositions within the semantic class of characterization (3.2.2.1):

> (17) *The Nicholsons, the people who had Tanya's bottom flat,* were freethinking and open-minded; they both invariably wore pink shirts. (SEU w.16.2.98–2)

However, this apposition (and others as well) were lacking in the fictional genre (4.4), largely because in a fictional text there is a different relationship between author (or narrator) and audience than there is in other kinds of written texts: as a fictional text unfolds, the reader and narrator come to share much personal knowledge about the fictional world being created – knowledge of characters, events, and so forth. In press reportage, in contrast, there is no such relationship between author and audience: an article in a newspaper, for instance, is relatively short and self-contained, and information about people and events must be presented immediately. Consequently, while there is a great need in press and learned writing for information to be supplied about individuals and events, in fictional texts there is little need to do so and therefore much less need for appositions.

4.3.2 *Variation within the spoken genres*

While the spoken genre in general contained fewer appositions than the learned and press genres, within the sub-genres of this genre there was considerable variation, variation resulting in part from the discourse participants in these sub-genres having varied degrees of shared personal knowledge. Fewer appositions occurred in the speech of equals and intimates – individuals who would possess a high degree of shared knowledge – than in the speech of disparates – individuals who would not possess a high degree of shared knowledge. However, just the opposite tendency was found in texts representing the speech of individuals who were both intimates and equals. Because these individuals share a high amount of personal knowledge, one would expect to find few appositions in their speech. But as Table 4.5 illustrates, their speech contained as many appositions as the speech of disparates. The unexpected high frequency of appositions in the speech of intimates/equals is probably the result of the relatively small size (30,000 words) of this part of the corpus and the increased likelihood, therefore, that the results could be skewed by unexpected variation within the small number of samples surveyed. And

Table 4.6. *Variation within genres of the corpora*

Genre	Fewest appos	Most appos	Difference	SD
Fiction	1.5	11.5	10.0	2.7
Conversation				
Intimates	3.6	8.0	4.4	1.4
Equals	3.8	7.2	3.4	1.3
Disparates	5.2	9.8	4.6	2.1
Intimates/equals	4.4	10.8	6.4	2.5
Learned				
Scientific	1.0	15.0	14.0	4.4
Humanistic	2.0	21.4	19.4	5.5
Press	3.5	25.0	21.5	5.1

indeed if one investigates the frequency of appositions in the individual samples of each genre, one finds considerable variation.

4.3.3 *Variation within individual genres*

Appendix 2 lists the number of appositions that occurred in each sample of the corpora. Table 4.6, which is based on information from Appendix 2, lists the fewest and most appositions occurring in the samples of each genre, and the standard deviation for each genre: the extent to which the mean scores for samples within a genre differ from one another.

Table 4.6 demonstrates that while there was variation within all genres, the most variation occurred in the learned and press genres, the least in the fiction and conversation genres. In the spontaneous conversation of intimates, for instance, the standard deviation was low (1.4), and there was little difference between the sample with the fewest apposition (3.6 per thousand words) and the sample with the most appositions (8.0). In the press genre, on the other hand, the variation was much more striking: the standard deviation was high (5.1), and the sample with the fewest appositions (3.5) contained far fewer appositions than the sample with the most appositions (25.0).

The variation present within the genres of the corpora has two explanations. First, as Biber (1988:170) observes, "Genres are not equally coherent in their linguistic characteristics..." A genre such as press reportage consists of many sub-genres: reportage, for instance, can cover such diverse areas as culture, politics, and sports (Biber 1988:191–2). And because these sub-genres are so different, Biber found many linguistic differences between them – differences that are attributable to the different functional needs of these sub-genres and the existence, therefore, of different linguistic constructions, such as appositions, to satisfy these needs. Second, although all appositions add to the flow of discourse, different appositions add to this flow in different ways and will therefore be better suited to some contexts than to others. This characteristic of appositions is an additional reason why there was variation in the corpora and will be explored in greater detail in the next section.

4.4 The frequency of occurrence of specific kinds of appositions in the genres of the corpora

In the previous section, it was demonstrated that because the second unit of an apposition provides new information about the first unit, appositions occurred most frequently in genres and sub-genres in which discourse participants possessed a low degree of shared personal knowledge. While this characteristic of appositions explains their variable occurrence in many genres of the corpora, it does not explain why, for instance, more appositions occurred in the learned humanistic genre than in the learned scientific genre – genres in which one would expect discourse participants to share equal amounts of personal knowledge and therefore to use appositions to a similar extent. To explain the variable occurrence of appositions in these and other genres, one must examine an additional characteristic of appositions: that certain kinds of appositions have specific communicative functions better suited to some genres than to others. For instance, appositions within the semantic class of appellation (example 18) occurred more frequently in the press genre than in the learned genre (4.4.2.3) because this kind of apposition satisfies a communicative need of press reportage: to identify and name individuals.

> (18) *A student teacher, Charles Woollett,* aged 19, of Banbury, Oxfordshire, was drowned last night when six canoes capsized in high seas off Blyth beach, Northumberland, during a Duke of Edinburgh award expedition. (SEU w.12.1–59)

In the corpora, the semantic classes of apposition and the syntactic forms used to realize these classes fell into two general categories: classes and forms that were distributed relatively evenly across the genres of the corpora because they had communicative functions well suited to all contexts, and classes and forms that were unevenly distributed because they had communicative functions suited only to specific contexts.

4.4.1 *Appositions occurring with equal frequency in the genres of the corpora*

As Table 4.7 illustrates, there were three semantic classes of appositions that were relatively evenly distributed among at least three of the four major genres of the corpora: the semantic classes of reorientation, particularization, and exemplification.[4] Relatively equal proportions of appositions

Table 4.7. *The semantic classes of reorientation, particularization, and exemplification in the genres of the corpora (numbers in parentheses indicate the number of appositions per thousand words)*

Genre	R	P	E
Fiction			
SEU	7 (0.2)	9 (0.2)	6 (0.2)
Brown	12 (0.3)	16 (0.4)	18 (0.5)
Total	19 (0.2)	25 (0.3)	24 (0.3)
Conversation			
Intimates	10 (0.3)	5 (0.2)	11 (0.4)
Equals	4 (0.1)	13 (0.4)	25 (0.8)
Disparates	12 (0.4)	22 (0.7)	21 (0.7)
Intimates/equals	6 (0.2)	9 (0.3)	23 (0.8)
Total	32 (0.3)	49 (0.4)	80 (0.7)
Learned			
Scientific (Brown)	6 (0.3)	7 (0.4)	6 (0.3)
Scientific (SEU)	5 (0.3)	13 (0.7)	25 (1.3)
Humanistic (Brown)	4 (0.3)	13 (0.7)	10 (0.5)
Humanistic (SEU)	1 (0.1)	6 (0.3)	15 (0.8)
Total	16 (0.2)	39 (0.5)	56 (0.7)
Press			
SEU	0 (0.0)	12 (0.3)	9 (0.2)
Brown	4 (0.1)	13 (0.3)	8 (0.2)
Total	4 (0.1)	25 (0.3)	17 (0.2)
Total	71 (0.2)	138 (0.4)	177 (0.5)

R = Reorientation
P = Particularization
E = Exemplification

within each of these classes occurred in the genres of fiction, conversation, and learned writing; few instances of each class occurred in the press genre. This distribution existed for two reasons. First, in press reportage, the most important communicative goal is naming individuals and attributing characteristics to them, communicative goals best accomplished by the semantic classes of, respectively, appellation and characterization. Hence, these classes of appositions predominated in the press genre (4.4.2.3) at the exclusion of the other semantic classes. Second, the semantic classes of reorientation, particularization, and exemplification are heterogeneous classes whose realizations are multi-functional and therefore appropriate, as Table 4.8 demonstrates, in a variety of the genres of the corpora. Some appositions in these classes contain second units whose function is to "clarify" either the reference or meaning of the first unit. Other appositions comprise second units whose function is to "focus" the reference of a very

Table 4.8. *Syntactic forms realizing the relations of reorientation, particularization, and exemplification* (*numbers in parentheses indicate the number of appositions per thousand words*)

Form	F	C	L	P
Reorientation				
NP (d)+NP (d)	14 (0.2)	23 (0.2)	5 (0.1)	0 (0.0)
Misc proper NP	4 (0.1)	4 (0.1)	0 (0.0)	0 (0.0)
Other	1 (0.01)	5 (0.1)	11 (0.2)	4 (0.1)
Particularization				
NP (i)+NP (i)	11 (0.1)	29 (0.2)	16 (0.2)	5 (0.1)
NP+partic+NP	7 (0.1)	10 (0.1)	19 (0.2)	19 (0.2)
Adjective phrase	6 (0.1)	4 (0.1)	2 (0.03)	0 (0.0)
Other	1 (0.03)	6 (0.1)	1 (0.01)	1 (0.01)
Exemplification				
NP+*like*+NP	15 (0.2)	70 (0.6)	14 (0.2)	6 (0.1)
NP+*such as*+NP	9 (0.1)	7 (0.1)	37 (0.5)	11 (0.1)
Other	0 (0.0)	3 (0.1)	5 (0.1)	0 (0.0)

F = Fiction
C = Conversation
L = Learned writing
P = Press writing

Table 4.9. *Appositions within the classes of reorientation and particularization serving a clarification function*

Class	F	C	L	P	Total
Reorientation	7 (12%)	32 (54%)	16 (27%)	4 (7%)	59
Partic.	12 (21%)	30 (53%)	12 (21%)	3 (5%)	57

F = Fiction
C = Conversation
L = Learned writing
P = Press writing

general first unit. Still other appositions consist of units whose parallel structures create "stylistic" effects.

4.4.1.1 *Appositions serving a clarification function*

A number of the forms in the semantic classes of reorientation and particularization contained second units whose function was to clarify either the reference or the meaning of the first unit. Because many of the second units in appositions of this type served to "edit" a misunderstanding created by the first unit, appositions of this type, as Table 4.9 illustrates, occurred predominantly in the genre of spontaneous conversation.

Examples 19–22 contain appositions within the semantic class of reorientation whose second units serve the purpose of clarifying the reference of the first unit. In example 19, the speaker makes clear in the second unit of the apposition that the RPM he referred to in the first unit is a forty-five disc.

> (19) *This little RPM, this little forty-five disc*, was our idea of the minimum desirable thing to get something across. (LLC s.3.2 943–6)

In example 20, the speaker simply names an individual in the first unit; in the second unit he refers to him as a professor in order to make clear the individual's status.

> (20) There is a scene in the college, a unit in the college, run by *Lev Mastine, Professor Mastine*, which is trying to arrange central timetabling in the college. (LLC s.3.4 517–24)

In example 21, the speaker initially refers to an individual by his first name. When she realizes, however, that the hearer does not understand whom she is talking about, she adds in the second unit of the apposition the individual's surname.

> (21) "We really ought to do something for him," Isabel said. "For whom?"
> "For *Alec – Mr Goodrich*." (SEU w.16.19–1)

In example 22, the second unit clarifies the fact that the address in the first unit refers to the White House.

> (22) Of course, *1600 Pennsylvania, the White House*, is the most famous address of the free world. (Brown A08 260–90)

While the second units in the above examples clarified the reference of the first units, in other appositions the second units clarified the intended meanings of the first units. Appositions of this type occurred in the semantic class of particularization, and were quite common in spontaneous conversation (see Table 4.9), largely because they are well suited to the spontaneous and unplanned nature of this kind of speech. The second unit of this kind of apposition contains the same head as the first unit and becomes a hyponym of the first unit through the addition of a modifier or intensifier. Consequently, this apposition allows a speaker to be more precise without having to think up an entirely different word for doing so. In example 23, the units of the apposition contain identical head noun phrases: *lectures*. Because this noun phrase is quite general, the speaker adds the modifier *department* to it in the second unit to clarify the fact that what he meant by lectures in the first unit was not just any lectures but lectures given in the department.

> (23) We don't have *any lectures, department lectures*, in the morning. (LLC s.33 251–2)

In example 24, the second unit of the apposition enables the speaker to stress the fact that he feels that Thorpe will not just be horrified but extremely horrified that the department does no work in language.

> (24) If I had to tell Thorpe we really don't do any language work there, he'd be *horrified, simply horrified*. (LLC s.1.6 201–4)

In example 25, speaker B uses the second unit of the apposition to note that he finds the professor he is discussing not just charming but absolutely charming.

> (25) A: I know him [Professor Kalapandy] by sight, and I've heard him lecture.
>
> B: [*A*] *charmer, an absolute charmer*, is Kalapandy, and a wonderful lecturer. (LLC s.1.6 1019–26)

4.4.1.2 *Appositions serving a focusing function*

Because the second units of the appositions in examples 19–25 clarified a misunderstanding created by the first units, these appositions tended to occur in a genre in which this type of "editing" would be tolerated: spontaneous conversation. Appositions serving a focusing function, however, tended to occur in all of the genres, since the function of these appositions – focusing the reference of a very general first unit – is a function appropriate in a variety of genres.

The semantic class of particularization contained one type of apposition whose second unit served a focusing function: appositions containing obligatory markers of apposition such as *particularly* and *especially*. These markers are members of a class of focusing subjuncts known as "particularizers," whose general function is to "draw attention to" constituents of varying complexity (Quirk *et al.* 1985:604). In appositions, particularizers mark the second unit of an apposition as containing a noun phrase whose reference is narrower than the first unit. So few appositions of this type occurred in the corpora that it is difficult to make precise generalizations about their distributions. Nevertheless, as Table 4.8 illustrates, these appositions occurred in all of the genres, with slightly more occurrences in the genres of learned writing and press writing.

Examples 26 and 27 illustrate the functions that this type of apposition can serve. In example 26, the second unit of the apposition, which is introduced by the particularizer *particularly*, narrows the reference of the first unit to make the writer's point that it is not just any historical novel or film that leaves a lasting impression but those seen during one's youth.

> (26) The clear pictures of historical situations or of characters provided by *historical novels or films*, particularly *those seen in youth*, often seem to leave a curiously lasting impression. (SEU w.9.3 6–4, 7–1)

In example 27, the second unit is introduced by the particularizer *especially*. This particularizer indicates that the second unit of the apposition will narrow the reference of the first unit and focus on specific individuals who will become poorer as others become richer: those individuals who are members of lower socio-economic groups.

> (27) As the rich got richer, *many of the poor* became poorer, especially *the members of the low castes or 'outcastes' like the Untouchables who had never had much land in the first place.* (SEU w.9.6 47–8)

In examples 26 and 27, particularizers served the function of focusing the reference of the first unit. In appositions within the class of exemplification, the second unit focuses the reference of the first unit by providing a representative example of it.

The relation of exemplification was most frequently realized by appositions containing the obligatory markers of apposition *like* and *such as* (Table 4.8). Typically these appositions consist of a first unit that is a very general indefinite or generic noun phrase and a second unit that is a definite noun phrase (2.1.3.1). The function of the second unit of these appositions, then, is to provide a concrete example of the first unit so that the listener or reader knows precisely what the speaker or writer is referring to in the first unit. In example 28, in the second unit of the apposition, the speaker names an individual so that the listener has a concrete example of one of the friends mentioned in the first unit.

> (28) I've got *friends* like *Peter Hammell*, who's a, uhm, art director. (LLC s.1.10 491–2)

In example 29, specific food items are given in the second unit to give the reader tangible examples of the non-edible items quite generally referred to in the first unit.

> (29) The bullocks need to be given some fodder, *mostly non-edible items from the farm* such as *rice hay, millet hay or cane leaves*, and they also graze on harvested fields or the village waste. (SEU w.9.6 54–5)

Overall in the corpora, as Table 4.8 demonstrates, the marker *like* was more common in this type of apposition than the marker *such as*. This distribution might reflect the feeling by some that *such as* is stylistically more cumbersome than *like* and that therefore "*Like* is often more comfortable than *such as*" (Copperud 1964:385). Table 4.8 also demonstrates that appositions containing the markers *like* and *such as* were distributed differently in the genres of conversation and learned writing. Appositions with the marker *like* occurred most frequently in conversation, those with *such as* most frequently in learned writing. The less frequent

Table 4.10. *The complexity of the second unit in appositions containing the markers* like *and* such as

Marker	One word	More than one word
Like	94 (90%)	11 (10%)
Such as	36 (57%)	27 (43%)

Table 4.11. *Appositions within the class of reorientation serving a stylistic function*

Class	F	C	L	P	Total
Reorientation	12	0	0	0	12

F = Fiction
C = Conversation
L = Learned writing
P = Press writing

occurrence of the marker *like* in learned writing might result from the general stigma now associated with the word *like* and the tendency, therefore, for *like* to be used less frequently in formal contexts such as learned writing. Initially, *like* was stigmatized only when it was used as a conjunction (e.g. *The woman looks like she's feeling ill*). Now, as Quirk *et al.* (1985:662) note, this stigma is often transferred to prepositional uses of *like*; and by extension, as the results of this study indicate, to uses of *like* as an obligatory marker of apposition. Related to the stigma attached to *like* is the belief that *such as* is preferable "if more than one example is mentioned, e.g. *British composers such as Elgar, Vaughan Williams, and Britten*" (*The Oxford Guide to the English Language*, p. 115). This claim was in general supported by the usage of *like* and *such as* in the corpora. As Table 4.10 indicates, if the second unit of an apposition consisted of a single phrase, it was more common for the marker *like* to be used than the marker *such as*.

4.4.1.3 *Appositions serving a stylistic function*
There was one final function that appositions within the semantic classes of reorientation could serve: a stylistic function. This function was realized by appositions whose units were definite noun phrases. As Table 4.11 shows, this kind of apposition occurred exclusively in the genre of fiction, a genre in which the stylistic effects created by such appositions would be most appropriate. In example 30, both units not only describe why Lady Foxglove disliked the individual referred to in the sentence but convey this

sentiment in the emphatic end-position of the sentence and in parallel constructions consisting of definite noun phrases postmodified by prepositional phrases beginning with *of*.

> (30) To Lady Foxglove he was *the personification of her husband's sin, the daily reminder of her failure as a wife and her gullibility as a woman.* (SEU w.16.3.199–1)

In example 31, the apposition in the last sentence of the passage consists of units whose parallelism and placement in the emphatic end-position of the sentence serve to emphasize the lawyer's happiness about the outcome of a trial.

> (31) At first Barco was evasive and shifty. But with Welch's relentless pursuit of the subject, Barco finally "broke" and started confessing to one murder after another. By the time Barco reached the count of three, the situation seemed to Welch almost too good to be true. But if true, it was *the case of which he had dreamed, the case which would throw him into headlines all over America as the hero of a great murder trial.* (Brown ROI 470–520)

In example 32, the parallel noun phrases that begin each unit of the apposition serve to emphasize the emotional upheaval experienced by the character being discussed in the passage.

> (32) He remembered very well *the heart-searchings of that summer, the times he had taken stock of his position.* (SEU w.16.7.26–2)

4.4.2 *Appositions occurring with unequal frequency in the genres of the corpora*

Because of the multi-functional nature of appositions within the semantic classes of reorientation, particularization, and exemplification, these classes were relatively evenly distributed across the genres of the corpora. The remaining semantic classes, however, had more specific functions and tended to predominate therefore in specific genres of the corpora.

4.4.2.1 *The distribution of appositions in the class of self-correction*

Appositions within the semantic class of self-correction contained a second unit whose function was to correct a mistake made by the speaker or writer in the first unit (3.2.3.3).[5] Because the mistakes present in the first units of these appositions would be edited out of writing, most appositions of this type occurred, as Table 4.12 illustrates, in the genre of spontaneous conversation.

Table 4.12. *The semantic class of self-correction in the genres of the corpora*

Genre	Number of appositions	Appositions per 1,000 words
Fiction		
SEU	2	0.05
Brown	1	0.03
Total	3	0.04
Conversation		
Intimates	10	0.3
Equals	10	0.3
Disparates	9	0.3
Intimates/equals	33	1.1
Total	62	0.5
Learned		
Scientific (Brown)	0	0.0
Scientific (SEU)	0	0.0
Humanistic (Brown)	0	0.0
Humanistic (SEU)	2	0.1
Total	2	0.03
Press		
SEU	2	0.05
Brown	0	0.0
Total	2	0.03
Total	69	0.2

In example 33, which contains a double apposition (2.3), the second units of each apposition, introduced by the marker *or*, correct successive mistakes the speaker makes.

> (33) We never shot *Haig*, or *French*, or *whoever the old fools were that we had there*. (LLC s.2.3 745–9)

In example 34, the second unit enables the speaker to correct an initial assertion he made, namely that he had met two, not one, Frenchmen.

> (34) I did know once *a Frenchman*, or *two Frenchmen*, really. (LLC s.1.6 414–17)

In example 35, which was taken from one of the written texts, the second unit allows the writer to assert that the book under discussion in the sentence will not provide the sole means but only part of the means of distinguishing certain kinds of expressions.

> (35) Such a book deals with many more differences in style of introduction than we are now concerned with. But among the

Table 4.13. *The semantic class of paraphrase in the genres of the corpora*

Genre	Number of appositions	Appositions per 1,000 words
Fiction		
SEU	59	1.5
Brown	66	1.7
Total	125	1.6
Conversation		
Intimates	55	1.8
Equals	61	2.0
Disparates	70	2.3
Intimates/equals	72	2.4
Total	258	2.2
Learned		
Scientific (Brown)	22	1.1
Scientific (SEU)	26	1.3
Humanistic (Brown)	49	2.5
Humanistic (SEU)	43	2.2
Total	140	1.8
Press		
SEU	15	0.4
Brown	28	0.7
Total	43	0.5
Total	566	1.6

differences it deals with is one which supplies us with *the means*, or *part of the means*, of distinguishing A-expressions and B-expressions. (SEU w.9.1.147–1)

4.4.2.2 *The distribution of appositions in the class of paraphrase*
Appositions within the semantic class of paraphrase contain a second unit that paraphrases the meaning of the first unit (3.2.3.1). As Table 4.13 illustrates, this class of apposition occurred most frequently in the conversation genre and slightly less frequently in the learned and fiction genres; relatively few instances occurred in the press genre.

Table 4.14 lists the syntactic forms that most frequently realized the relation of paraphrase and their frequency of occurrence in the genres of the corpora. As this table illustrates, the relation of paraphrase is realized by appositions containing either synonymous clauses or synonymous phrases, and these realizations had quite different distributions in the genres of the corpora: appositions containing two sentences predominated in the conversation genre, those containing noun phrases in the learned and fiction genres. All appositions within the class of paraphrase have a similar function: "to preclude uncertainty or contest" (de Beaugrande and Dressler 1981:80), that is, to insure that the hearer or reader understands the meaning of a proposition or phrase introduced into the discourse as the first unit of the apposition. However, as Table 4.14 illustrates, it was more important in conversation for propositions to be defined, and more important in learned writing and fiction for phrases to be defined.[6]

In conversation, appositions containing units that are sentences are communicatively important because they enable the speaker to expand upon the meaning of a proposition that he or she feels the hearer might not fully understand. In example 36, the speaker uses the second unit of the apposition to explain precisely how authorities are not recruiting to capacity.

> (36) Many authorities now are not recruiting to capacity. That is to say, when you get a school that, say, has got twenty teachers, when one of them dies or retires or moves on they'll soldier on with nineteen. (LLC s.3.2 532–59)

In example 37, the speaker explains in the second unit of the apposition exactly why his department is small.

> (37) We're a small department. [That is to say] we've only three lecturers. (LLC s.1.6 207–8)

In example 38, the speaker defines in the second unit what she means by German precision.

> (38) I'm getting absolutely German with my precision. [That is to say] I can't bear things to be in a mess. (LLC s.2.10 978–9)

These kinds of appositions, as Table 4.14 demonstrates, did not occur exclusively in conversation: some occurred in learned writing as well, a genre in which it is also necessary to define the meaning of a proposition, especially if it is complex. In example 39, the writer paraphrases in the second unit of the apposition what he means by his assertion that internal energy depends only on temperature.

> (39) The internal energy of an ideal gas depends on temperature only and is independent of pressure or volume. In other words, if an ideal gas is compressed and kept at constant temperature, the work done in compressing it is completely converted into heat and transferred to the surrounding heat sink. (Brown J03 1610–50)

While it is communicatively important in conversation that the meaning of propositions be made clear, in writing it is more important, as Table 4.14 demonstrates, that the meaning of phrases be made clear. Lexically, there

Table 4.14. *Syntactic forms realizing the relation of paraphrase*

Form	F	C	L	P	Total
Clausal paraphrase					
Sentence	35 (0.4)	159 (1.3)	47 (0.6)	18 (0.2)	259 (0.7)
Subordinate clause	16 (0.2)	15 (0.1)	21 (0.3)	5 (0.1)	57 (0.2)
Other	12 (0.2)	21 (0.2)	4 (0.1)	2 (0.02)	39 (0.1)
Total	63 (0.8)	195 (1.6)	72 (0.9)	25 (0.3)	355 (1.0)
Phrasal paraphrase					
NP (i) + NP (i)	33 (0.4)	26 (0.2)	24 (0.3)	8 (0.1)	91 (0.3)
Adj phrase	9 (0.1)	15 (0.1)	9 (0.1)	0 (0.0)	33 (0.1)
Other	20 (0.3)	22 (0.2)	35 (0.4)	10 (0.1)	87 (0.2)
Total	62 (0.8)	63 (0.5)	68 (0.9)	18 (0.2)	211 (0.6)
Total	125 (1.6)	258 (2.2)	140 (1.8)	43 (0.5)	566 (1.6)

F = Fiction
C = Conversation
L = Learned writing
P = Press writing
i = indefinite

Table 4.15. *Types of semantic relations between phrases realizing the class of paraphrase*

Relation	F	C	L (s)	L (h)	P	Total
Absolute synonymy	15 (0.2)	16 (0.1)	28 (0.7)	12 (0.3)	5 (0.1)	76 (0.2)
Speaker synonymy	47 (0.6)	47 (0.4)	3 (0.1)	25 (0.6)	13 (0.2)	135 (0.4)
Total	62 (0.8)	63 (0.5)	31 (0.8)	37 (0.9)	18 (0.2)	211 (0.6)

F = Fiction
C = Conversation
L = Learned writing (s = scientific, h = humanistic)
P = Press writing

are two kinds of synonymy: absolute synonymy and speaker synonymy (3.1.2.1). As Table 4.15 illustrates, appositions exhibiting both kinds of synonymy had quite different distributions in the genres of the corpora: appositions whose units exhibited absolute synonymy predominated in learned scientific writing, those whose units exhibited speaker synonymy in fiction and learned humanistic writing.

Appositions whose units were absolutely synonymous predominated in the learned scientific genre because it is often important in this genre for scientists to give precise definitions of important terms that they introduce.

In example 40, the writer defines in the second unit of the apposition what the technical term *autosuggestibility* means.

> (40) *Autosuggestibility, the reaction of the subject in such a way as to conform to his own expectations of the outcome* (i.e., that the arm-rise is a reaction to the pressure exerted in the voluntary contraction, because of his knowledge that "to every reaction there is an equal and opposite reaction"), also seems inadequate as an explanation for the following reasons...(Brown J28 730–90)

In example 41, the writer uses the second unit of the apposition to define his use of the term *tanks*.

> (41) Paddy rice cultivation was restricted to flooded valley bottoms and a few patches of land capable of being irrigated from "*tanks*", [i.e.] *reservoirs formed by damming ephemeral streams*. (SEU w.9.6.35)

In example 42, the writer takes a slightly different approach to defining a term. Instead of introducing the technical term first and the more familiar synonym second, the writer reverses the order, first giving the familiar word (*third*) and then its technical equivalent (*pineal*).

> (42) On the dorsal side is a single nasal opening, and behind this there is a gap in the pigment layers of the skin through which the *third* or *pineal* eye can be seen as a yellow spot. (SEU w.9.7.84–2)

Because the appositions in examples 40–42 contain instances of absolute synonymy, they illustrate the importance in scientific writing of providing objective definitions of terms that one uses. In fiction and learned humanistic writing, on the other hand, this kind of objectivity is not as important. Consequently, it was much more common in these kinds of writing to find appositions whose units were related by the relation of speaker synonymy (see Table 4.15). This is a much more subjective kind of synonymy in the sense that the units of the apposition are not synonymous in the dictionary sense but in the sense that the writer wishes the units to be interpreted as synonymous. In example 43, the writer does not define a murderer objectively as someone who kills but rather makes the subjective assertion that a murderer is "a man of blood."

> (43) During the Brown trial, however, the state's most powerful Democratic newspaper, the *Providence Daily Post*, stated that Brown was *a murderer, a man of blood*, and that he and his associates, with the assistance of Republicans and Abolitionists, had plotted not only the liberation of the slaves but also the overthrow of state and federal governments. (Brown J58 20–80)

In example 44, the writer describes the Old Testament rather generally as being inspirational and prophetically important. In the second unit of the apposition, she defines precisely what she means by this assertion.

> (44) It [the Old Testament] was *an inspiration with prophetic importance: a pointing to the last days when God would speak by His Son.* (SEU w.9.2.136–3)

In example 45, the narrator defines quite impressionistically what grey vapour is.

> (45) The green air thinned to the width of a sword-blade that had just sliced clean the base of the heavy cumulus above it, and then suddenly was itself smashed to atoms, glowing round the wispy edges of *grey vapour – bright bits of lime-colour that grew smaller and smaller until they were stamped out into nothing by the cold blackness of continuous cloud.* (SEU w.16.4.45–1)

In example 46, the narrator equates a building's being shabby with its being dismal.

> (46) The address was in the Holborn district; it sounded *shabby, dismal.* (SEU w.16.1.19–1)

4.4.2.3 *The distribution of appositions in the classes of appellation and characterization*

As Table 4.16 indicates, appositions within the classes of appellation and characterization occurred most frequently in the press genre and much less frequently in the other genres. These distributions reflect both the close interrelationship between the classes of appellation and characterization and the fact that their communicative functions are well suited to the press genre.

Syntactically, the classes of appellation and characterization are very interrelated.[7] In appositions within the class of appellation (3.2.1.2), the second unit names the first unit (example 47). If the units of this type of apposition are reversed, the resultant apposition (example 48) is one within the class of characterization (3.2.2.1), a class in which the second unit attributes general characteristics to the first unit.

> (47) The Richard S. Burkes' home in Wayne may be the setting for the wedding reception for *their daughter, Helen Lambert,* and the young Italian she met last year while studying in Florence during her junior year at Smith College. (Brown A16 840–70)

> (48) The Richard S. Burkes' home in Wayne may be the setting for the wedding reception for *Helen Lambert, their daughter…*

Table 4.17 lists the syntactic forms that realized the relations of appellation and characterization and their frequency in the genres of the

Table 4.16. *The semantic classes of appellation and characterization in the genres of the corpora*

Genre	A	C
Fiction		
SEU	24 (0.6)	35 (0.9)
Brown	19 (0.4)	40 (1.0)
Total	43 (0.5)	75 (0.9)
Conversation		
Intimates	1 (0.03)	11 (0.4)
Equals	7 (0.2)	9 (0.3)
Disparates	8 (0.3)	4 (0.1)
Intimates/equals	5 (0.2)	13 (0.4)
Total	21 (0.2)	37 (0.3)
Learned		
Scientific (Brown)	2 (0.1)	6 (0.3)
Scientific (SEU)	6 (0.3)	17 (0.9)
Humanistic (Brown)	12 (0.6)	15 (0.8)
Humanistic (SEU)	5 (0.3)	6 (0.3)
Total	25 (0.3)	44 (0.6)
Press		
SEU	89 (2.2)	147 (3.7)
Brown	179 (4.4)	147 (3.7)
Total	268 (3.4)	294 (3.7)
Total	357 (1.0)	450 (1.25)

A = Appellation
C = Characterization

corpora. As this table demonstrates, most of these forms occurred in the press genre, and most contained a proper noun phrase as either the first or the second unit of the apposition. These forms predominated in the press genre because individuals are of prime importance in press reportage, and the classes of appellation and characterization help fulfill an important communicative function in this genre: naming and attributing characteristics to individuals about whom the reading public has little knowledge. And these appositions allow journalists flexibility in conveying this information.

Example 49 provides an illustration of the complementary function of appositions within the classes of appellation and characterization. As this excerpt demonstrates, these appositions allow writers to focus one of the units of the apposition and to convey information about individuals in a varied and non-monotonous manner. The excerpt begins with two appositions in the class of appellation which allow the writer to name both the coach of the team being discussed and two athletes he has recruited.

Table 4.17. *The syntactic forms realizing the relations of appellation and characterization*

Form	F	C	L	P	Total
Appellation					
NP (d) + proper NP	32 (0.4)	7 (0.1)	17 (0.2)	111 (1.4)	167
NP (−det) + proper NP	3 (0.04)	2 (0.03)	2 (0.03)	95 (B 2.4) 28 (SEU 0.7)	129
NP (i) + proper NP	5 (0.1)	9 (0.1)	6 (0.1)	31 (0.4)	51
Other	3 (0.04)	4 (0.03)	0 (0.0)	3 (0.04)	10
Characterization					
Proper NP + NP (−det)	1 (0.01)	0 (0.0)	2 (0.01)	62 B (1.5) 56 (SEU 1.4)	121
Proper NP + NP (d)	16 (0.2)	13 (0.2)	7 (0.1)	58 (0.7)	94
Proper NP + NP (i/a)	10 (0.1)	4 (0.03)	3 (0.03)	64 (0.8)	81
NP (d) + NP (i/a)	13 (0.2)	5 (0.04)	8 (0.1)	9 (0.1)	35
Other	35 (0.4)	16 (0.1)	24 (0.3)	45 (0.6)	120

NP (d) = definite noun phrase
NP (−det) = noun phrase lacking determiner
NP (i) = indefinite noun phrase
NP (i/a) = indefinite attributive noun phrase
F = Fiction   B = Brown Corpus
C = Conversation   SEU = Survey of English Usage Corpus
L = Learned writing
P = Press writing

Because the third apposition contains old information (*Rabb*, who is named at the end of the second apposition), this information is placed in the first unit of the apposition, resulting in an apposition in the class of characterization. The fourth apposition is parallel in structure to the third apposition and contains an apposition in which the second unit provides general descriptive information about a team that is introduced into the discourse, the Houston Oilers. The fifth apposition, however, breaks this pattern and contains an apposition in which the second unit names an athlete (*Jack Spikes*) who was unable to play in the game.

(49) [1] *Buffalo coach Buster Ramsey*, who has become one of the game's greatest collectors of quarterbacks, apparently now has found a productive pair in [2] *two ex-National Football Leaguers, M. C. Reynolds and Warren Rabb.*

[3] *Rabb, the former Louisiana State field general,* came off the bench for his debut with the Bills Sunday and directed his new team to a 22–12 upset victory over [4] *the Houston Oilers, defending league champions.*

"Just our luck!" exclaimed Stram. "Buster would solve that quarterback problem just as we head that way."

Ramsey has a thing or two to mutter about himself, for the Dallas defensive unit turned in another splendid effort against Denver, and the Texans were able to whip the dangerous Broncs without the fullbacking of [5] *a top star, Jack Spikes,* though he did the team's place-kicking while nursing a knee injury. (Brown A12 1330–50)

Table 4.17 also reveals that two forms realizing the relations of appellation and characterization occurred almost exclusively in the press genre. Both forms contained a unit lacking a determiner, either in the first unit (example 50) or in the second unit (example 51).

(50) *Incumbent Richard Salter* seeks re-election and is opposed by Donald Huffman for the five-year term. (Brown A10 1080–90)

(51) *Mr. Selwyn Lloyd, Leader of the Commons,* will have to revise his parliamentary timetable to fill the gap between now and the summer recess. (SEU w.12.2.7)

These kinds of appositions predominated in the press genre, largely because of the importance of concision in journalistic writing: the need to convey information in as economical a form as possible.[8]

Another difference represented in Table 4.17 concerned the use in British and American English of appositions containing a "pseudo-title" (Bell 1988) followed by a proper noun phrase (2.5.4.1):

(52) *Rookie southpaw George Stepanovich* relieved Hyde at the start of the ninth and gave up the A's fifth tally on a walk to *second baseman Dick Howser,* a wild pitch, and Frank Cipriani's single under *shortstop Jerry Adair*'s glove into center. (Brown A11 220–50)

This kind of apposition, as Table 4.17 illustrates, occurred almost exclusively in the press genre. However, it was much more common in the American corpus than in the British corpus. As Table 4.18 documents, 16 of the 20 samples from the Brown Corpus contained more than two instances of appositions of the type in example 52. In contrast, only 3 of the 8 samples from the SEU Corpus contained more than two instances of this type of apposition. These findings confirm Bell's (1988:337) observation that appositions containing pseudo-titles are "the norm" in American press writing and are "not identified with any class of media."

In the British media, on the other hand, the use of this kind of apposition is disputed. While British style guides such as Greenbaum and Whitcut (1988:270) claim that such appositions are "useful to journalists...[they] do not belong in ordinary writing." Many newspaper style manuals,

Table 4.18. *Appositions containing pseudo-titles in the press genre*

Frequency	Brown	SEU
No instances	1	2
One instance	3	3
Two or more instances	16	3

Table 4.19. *Appositions containing pseudo-titles in specific British newspapers*

SAMPLE	Newspaper	No. of pseudo-titles
W.12.1	Times	1
W.12.2	Daily Express	8
W.12.3	Guardian	0
W.12.4	Daily Telegraph	0
W.12.5	Guardian (sports)	2
W.12.6	Daily Telegraph Financial Times	1
W.12.7	Misc	15
W.12.8	Misc	1

however, are less tolerant of their usage. *The Independent Style Manual*, for instance, prohibits the use of appositions containing pseudo-titles, claiming that "people's jobs are not titles" (p. 6). This guide advises its users to place the individual's job description in the second unit instead:

> (53) SIR EDWARD BOYLE, *Minister of Education*, said in Birmingham that the part-time woman teacher must be accepted as an increasingly important factor in school life. (SEU W.12.1–29)

But interestingly, as Table 4.17 illustrates, appositions of this type did not occur any more frequently in the British corpus than the American corpus.

Because of the stigma associated with the use of appositions containing pseudo-titles, these constructions, as both Allen (1988) and Rydén (1975) have documented, tend to be avoided in more learned and prestigious British newspapers and to be restricted in use to less formal and more popular British newspapers. This tendency, as Table 4.19 indicates, was evident in the newspapers included in the SEU Corpus. More formal newspapers, such as *The Times*, *The Guardian*, *The Daily Telegraph*, and *The Financial Times*, contained virtually no instances of this kind of apposition. On the other hand, more popular newspapers, such as *The Daily Express*, contained more instances of appositions with pseudo-titles.

Table 4.20. *The class of identification in the genres of the corpora*

Genre	Number of appositions	Appositions per 1,000 words
Fiction		
SEU	59	1.5
Brown	72	1.8
Total	131	1.6
Conversation		
Intimates	55	1.8
Equals	40	1.3
Disparates	77	2.6
Intimates/equals	67	2.2
Total	239	2.0
Learned		
Scientific (Brown)	83	4.2
Scientific (SEU)	105	5.3
Humanistic (Brown)	77	3.9
Humanistic (SEU)	167	8.4
Total	432	5.4
Press		
SEU	120	3.0
Brown	91	2.3
Total	211	2.6
Total	1,013	2.8

Status, then, is the main difference between the use of this type of apposition in British and American newspapers: while an apposition of the type in example 54 would be stylistically unmarked in an American newspaper, in British newspapers it is associated with "tabloid" journalism.

> (54) *Calverton miner Sydney Gilliburn* was today hailed as a fire
> hero after rescuing his family, saving the life of his son and then
> tackling a blaze single-handed. (SEU w.12.7.1–2)

4.4.2.4 *The distribution of appositions in the class of identification*
While the semantic classes of appellation and characterization occurred mainly in the press genre, the semantic class of identification, as Table 4.20 demonstrates, occurred in all genres but with slightly greater frequency in the learned genre.

Appositions within the class of identification consist of a second unit that is more specific than the first unit and that identifies the referent of the first unit (3.2.1.1). In example 55, the second unit identifies the particular cash crops mentioned in the first unit.

Table 4.21. *The syntactic forms realizing the relation of identification*

Form	F	C	L	P	Total
NP + clause/sentence	36 (0.5)	97 (0.8)	130 (1.6)	119 (1.5)	382
Citations/titles	7 (0.1)	10 (0.1)	122 (1.5)	20 (0.3)	159
NP + *of* + NP/clause	15 (0.2)	23 (0.2)	38 (0.5)	14 (0.2)	90
Numbers/symbols	1 (0.01)	1 (0.01)	60 (0.8)	12 (0.2)	74
Other	72 (0.9)	108 (0.9)	82 (1.0)	46 (0.6)	308

F = Fiction
C = Conversation
L = Learned writing
P = Press writing

(55) The current rich farmers in Wangala are peasant men who had enterprise, enough land, and a little working capital, and who, in 1939, discovered suddenly an opportunity to make large profits out of *the new cash crops, sugar cane and rice.* (SEU w.9.6.45–6).

Providing more specific information about a fairly general first unit is a communicative act that would be appropriate in a variety of contexts. Therefore, it is not surprising that this type of apposition occurred in all genres of the corpora. However, more appositions of this type occurred in the learned genre than the other genres for two primary reasons.

First, as Table 4.21 illustrates, three of the more frequently occurring appositions in the class of identification contained syntactic forms quite common in learned writing: a noun phrase in apposition with a clause or sentence (example 56), a linguistic citation (example 57), and a measurement (example 58).

(56) If barbarous nations have been barbarous because it was their nature so to be, then, if they become independent, they will slowly or quickly sink back into barbarism, and it is no good acting on *the assumption that they will do anything else.* (SEU w.9.3 5–1)

(57) It [the remark] is as empty as *the word "Hurrah"* would be when there was no enthusiasm behind it. (Brown J52 1080–100)

(58) It was shown that correction for secondary extinction was only necessary for *intense reflections*, namely *(310) and (400)*, measured with the cO axis vertical. (SEU w.9.8.170–1)

Appositions containing measurements, citations, numbers, and symbols were infrequent in the conversation and press genres, largely because these forms are ill suited to these genres: in casual conversation, the topic of discussion is usually informal; in press reportage, individuals are the primary focus, and appositions containing proper nouns are restricted to occurring in the classes of appellation and characterization (4.4.2.3). Although appositions containing a noun phrase in apposition with a clause or sentence were common in the press genre as well as the learned genre, they were quite uncommon in the fiction and conversation genres, largely because many of these appositions contain an abstract nominalized noun phrase in the first unit (2.1.2.1), and abstract noun phrases, as Biber (1988:154) observes, are uncommon in conversation and fiction, which tend to have "concrete, active emphases."

A second reason that appositions in the class of identification predominated in the learned genre is that many of the syntactic forms that realized the relation of identification were restricted to occurring in the class of identification: there was not, as was the case with appositions in the classes of appellation and characterization, a strong interrelationship between appositions in the class of identification and those in other classes. For instance, the units in the apposition in example 55 can be reversed, yielding an apposition within the class of characterization:

> (59) The current rich farmers in Wangala...discovered suddenly an opportunity to make large profits out of *sugar cane and rice, the new cash crops.*

However, none of the units in examples 56–58 can be reversed:

> (60) ?It was shown that correction for secondary extinction was only necessary for (310) and (400), intense reflections...

> (61) ?It [the remark] is as empty as "Hurrah," the word...

> (62) *...it is no good acting on that they will do anything else, the assumption.

Because of syntactic restrictions on the ordering of units in appositions such as the above, writers are restricted to using appositions within the class of identification and have few opportunities to vary their style and use appositions within the class of characterization.

5   Apposition in the grammar of English

The previous three chapters described the syntactic, semantic, and pragmatic characteristics that typify units in apposition. In this chapter, apposition is considered within the context of the grammar of English.

As Chapters 2 and 3 demonstrated, appositions have a variety of different syntactic and semantic characteristics. However, some of these characteristics are more common than others, making apposition a relation in which certain syntactic and semantic characteristics are dominant (5.1). Because apposition is such a linguistically diverse relation, appositions have, as Chapter 4 illustrated, a variety of different communicative functions, functions which vary mainly by genre rather than dialect (5.2): in the corpora there was little variation in the use of appositions in the samples containing written British and written American English, but considerable variation in the use of appositions in spoken and written English and in different genres of written English. Apposition is also a gradable relation, and if appositions are ranked according to their positions on the syntactic and semantic gradients of apposition, some appositions are centrally appositional, others only peripherally appositional (5.3). Finally, apposition is one of the more important grammatical relations in English, occurring considerably more frequently than most other grammatical relations, such as coordination and complementation (5.4).

5.1 The predominance of certain syntactic and semantic characteristics of apposition

Even though appositions have a variety of different syntactic and semantic characteristics, some of these characteristics occurred much more frequently in the corpora than others.

5.1.1 *Syntactic characteristics*

Syntactically, apposition is most commonly a relation between two juxtaposed noun phrases having a syntactic function (such as direct object) promoting end-weight.

Although units in apposition can have a variety of different syntactic forms (2.1), the majority of appositions in the corpora (66 percent) consisted of units that were noun phrases:

> (1) Desegregation is beginning in *two more important Southern cities – Dallas and Atlanta.* (Brown B09 850–60)

Because appositions are syntactically heavy constructions (2.2), most (65 percent) had functions that promote end-weight, most commonly direct object (example 2) or object of preposition (example 3).

> (2) A plug and a tube with holes in its cylindrical walls divided the chamber above the porous plug into two parts. This arrangement had *the purpose to prevent heated gas to reach the thermocouple by natural convection.* (Brown J02 900–30)

> (3) The heart is suspended in *a special portion of the coelom, the pericardium,* whose walls are supported by cartilage. (SEU W.9.7.91–1)

While the units of an apposition can be juxtaposed (example 4) or unjuxtaposed (example 5), most appositions (89 percent) were juxtaposed (2.3).

> (4) In her letter to John Brown, *"E.B.", the Quakeress from Newport,* had suggested that the American people owed more honor to John Brown for seeking to free the slaves than they did to George Washington. (Brown J58 1040–70)

> (5) That's *jolly brave,* I think, *jolly enterprising.* (LLC s.2.10 876–7)

Even though more than two units can be in apposition (2.3), most appositions (92 percent) were single appositions consisting of only two units (examples 4 and 5). In those rare instances when more than two units were in apposition, most units (70 percent) were in a binary rather than a non-binary relationship with one another (2.4). In example 6, the units are in a binary relationship because the last unit (*Britt Ekland*) is in apposition with the unit immediately preceding it (*Swedish star*); these units, in turn, are in apposition with the first unit of the apposition (*his bride of two months*):

> (6) Sellers was able to talk, even joke, today with *his bride of two months – Swedish star Britt Ekland,* who has been by his bedside almost constantly during the crisis hours. (SEU W.12.2.17)

5.1.2 *Semantic characteristics*

Semantically, appositions typically contain constructions that are referentially related and comprised of a second unit that adds greater specificity to the interpretation of the first unit.

While the units of an apposition can be referentially or non-referentially related (3.1), most appositions (62 percent) were related by some kind of referential relationship, most frequently coreference (example 7) or cataphoric reference (example 8).

> (7) Jean Fardulli's Blue Angel is the first top local club to import *that crazy new dance, the Twist.* (Brown A16 1880–900)

> (8) In order to remove the present uncertainties about the date of the General Election the Prime Minister thinks it right to inform the country of *his decision not to ask the Queen to dissolve Parliament before the autumn.* (SEU w.12.2–3)

Appositions can also be classified into various semantic classes depending upon whether the second unit of the apposition provides information about the first unit that is more specific, less specific, or equally specific (3.2). However, most appositions (59 percent) occurred in semantic classes that were more specific, semantic classes such as identification, in which the second unit identifies the referent of the first unit (example 9), or exemplification, in which the second unit provides an example of the first unit (example 10).

> (9) Well, Fan has a very smooth eldest son by *the name* of *Don* who married a very wealthy young woman. (LLC s.1.13 675–7)

> (10) *Some good judges* like *Lord Haldane* thought that it [the German General Staff] was never much good after eighteen seventy. (LLC s.2.3 373–5)

5.2 Dialect and genre variation in the use of appositions

In their study of vocabulary frequencies in the Brown Corpus and the London–Oslo–Bergen Corpus, Johansson and Hofland (1989:17) found that the "rank order of word classes" in written British and American English was "almost identical" but that there was considerable variation in the frequency of vocabulary within individual genres of British and American English. This finding leads Johansson and Hofland to conclude "that the major differences in word-class distribution are related to genre rather than dialect." If the distribution of appositions in the corpora of this study are compared, a similar pattern emerges: apposition usage varied little in comparable genres of written British and American English but considerably within individual genres of these varieties.

To demonstrate this variation in the use of appositions, three major linguistic characteristics of apposition were compared according to their frequency of occurrence in the three corpora used in this study – the Brown Corpus, the Survey of English Usage (SEU) Corpus, and the London–Lund Corpus (LLC) – and in three of the major genres of the corpora:

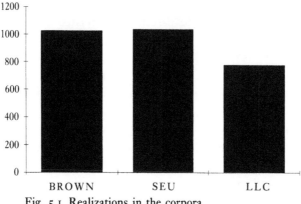

Fig. 5.1 Realizations in the corpora

press, learned writing, and fiction.[1] These comparisons illustrate that variation in apposition usage is motivated not by differences between American and British English but by the varying functional needs of the different genres of English.

5.2.1 *Realizations*

Figure 5.1 lists the number of constructions realizing the relation of apposition in the three corpora. As this figure illustrates, relatively equal numbers of appositions occurred in Brown and SEU; significantly fewer appositions occurred in LLC. Fewer appositions were present in speech than in writing because appositions are, in general, communicatively more necessary in writing than in speech (4.3).

Figure 5.2 outlines the occurrence of appositions in the written genres of the corpora and illustrates that these genres contained unequal numbers of appositions: most appositions occurred in the press genre with decreasing numbers of appositions in the genres of learned writing and fiction. Appositions occurred so frequently in the press genre because they are a useful grammatical construction in this genre for providing information about individuals discussed in press reportage (4.4.2.3).

5.2.2 *Syntactic forms*

Figure 5.3 details the occurrence in the corpora of the four primary syntactic forms that units in apposition have. As this figure shows, while the syntactic forms were relatively evenly distributed in Brown and SEU, there were significant differences in LLC. While most appositions in Brown and SEU were nominal appositions, relatively equal numbers of appositions in LLC were nominal as well as non-nominal appositions. Because noun

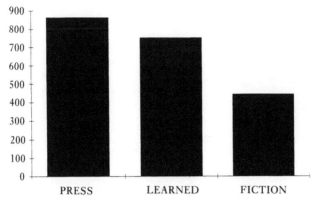
Fig. 5.2 Realizations in the written genres

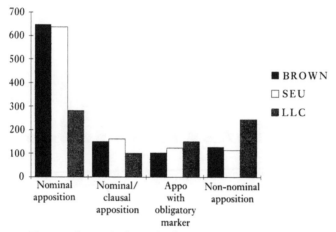
Fig. 5.3 Syntactic forms in the corpora

phrases tend to be less complex in spoken English than in written English (2.1.2), LLC had the fewest number of appositions containing a noun phrase in apposition with a clause or sentence. In addition, LLC contained slightly more instances of appositions having obligatory markers of apposition, largely because of the preponderance in this corpus of appositions containing the marker *like* (4.4.1.2).

Figure 5.4 illustrates the occurrence of the four syntactic forms in the written genres of the corpora. This figure demonstrates considerable variation among the genres. The press genre contained the most nominal appositions and the fewest non-nominal appositions because of the preponderance in the press genre of nominal appositions centred around proper nouns (4.4.2.3). The fiction genre contained the fewest appositions consisting of a noun phrase followed by a nominal clause. This distribution is a consequence of the fact that fictional texts are less likely to contain the

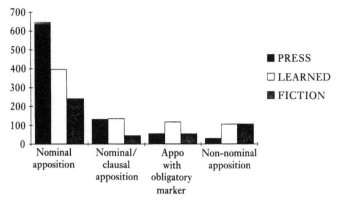

Fig. 5.4 Syntactic forms in the written genres

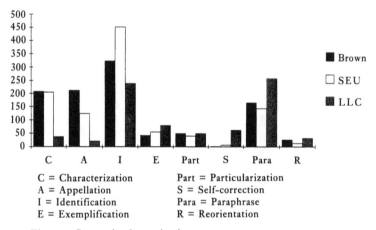

C = Characterization   Part = Particularization
A = Appellation   S = Self-correction
I = Identification   Para = Paraphrase
E = Exemplification   R = Reorientation

Fig. 5.5 Semantic classes in the corpora

abstract nominalized nouns that typify the first units of this type of apposition (cf. 2.1.2.1 and 4.4.2.4).

5.2.3 *Semantic classes*

Figure 5.5 lists the distribution in the corpora of appositions within particular semantic classes. While the semantic classes were distributed quite differently in LLC than in Brown and SEU, there was some variation in their distribution in Brown and SEU as well. This variation, however, was the only major variation in the use of appositions in British and American English.

There were two major areas in which apposition usage in Brown and SEU varied. Brown contained more instances than SEU of appositions in the class of appellation, largely because of the stigma in British English against certain kinds of restrictive appositions in this class (4.4.2.3):

(11) *Circuit Judge Paul R. Cash* did not set a date for sentencing. (Brown A20 260–70)

SEU contained more appositions in the class of identification than Brown because a couple of samples in SEU contained a disproportionate number of one kind of syntactic form in this class: linguistic citations (4.4.2.4):

(12) *The words 'stand for' and 'about'*, then, will not carry the explanatory weight which Geach's definitions require them to carry. (SEU w.9.1.145–3)

Aside from these two differences, however, the other semantic classes were quite evenly distributed in Brown and SEU, and quite unevenly in LLC.

Very few appositions in the classes of characterization and appellation occurred in LLC, largely because these appositions serve functions – attributing characteristics to or naming the first unit of an apposition – that are not important in speech (4.4.2.3). LLC contained fewer appositions in the class of identification than did Brown and SEU and more appositions in the class of paraphrase because of the greater number of non-nominal appositions in LLC (4.4.2.2), appositions which contain a second unit paraphrasing the meaning of the first unit:

(13) That [the book] is only for home consumption. [That is to say] It's not published. (LLC s.3.2 1055–6)

Virtually no appositions in the class of self-correction occurred in Brown and SEU because of the inappropriateness in writing of these kinds of appositions (4.4.2.1):

(14) I was going to this little beer off, down by Dick's new place, you know, down *Vintage Road*, [or] *Tenterden Road*, and this chap was charging twenty-one. (LLC s.1.7 465–70)

While there was considerable variation in the occurrence of semantic classes in written and spoken English, there was even greater variation, as Figure 5.6 demonstrates, in their occurrence in the written genres. Most of the appositions in the classes of characterization and appellation occurred in the press genre because of the communicative need in this genre to name individuals and attribute characteristics to them (4.4.2.3). In contrast, the learned style contained most of the appositions in the class of identification, largely because this style contained numerous syntactic forms (such as numbers and percentages) well suited to the class of identification (4.4.2.4):

(15) To purchase the remainder of its food at *the Middle Peasant standard (15.29 MJ per rupee)* would cost 163 rupees per caput, yet Epstein's surveys show that the total cash income of Untouchable households (most from wages) averaged only 207 rupees per caput! (SEU w.9.6.69)

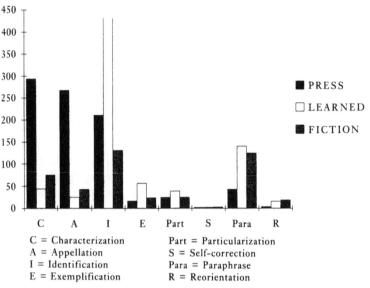

C = Characterization   Part = Particularization
A = Appellation   S = Self-correction
I = Identification   Para = Paraphrase
E = Exemplification   R = Reorientation

Fig. 5.6 Semantic classes in the written genres

The learned style contained the most instances of appositions in the classes of exemplification, particularization, and paraphrase because of the importance in this style of either focusing (example 16) or defining (example 17) the first unit of the apposition.

> (16) When we look at *countries* like *Iran, Iraq, Pakistan, and Burma*, where substantial progress has been made in creating a minimum supply of modern men and of social overhead capital, and where institutions of centralized government exist, we find a second category of countries with a different set of problems and hence different priorities for policy. (Brown J22 360–410)

> (17) When the smaller facet-planes of Analytical Cubism were placed upon or juxtaposed with the large, dense shapes formed by the affixed material of the collage, they had to *coalesce – become "synthesized"* – into larger planar shapes themselves simply in order to maintain the integrity of the picture plane. (Brown J59 1360–410)

5.3 Apposition as a gradable relation

Although a variety of constructions are considered appositions in this study, not all of these constructions are equally appositional (cf. 2.5 and 3.4): some constructions are central appositions, others peripheral appositions; still other constructions fall somewhere in between these two extremes.

Figure 5.7 lists the syntactic and semantic characteristics that determine whether a construction is a central or a peripheral apposition. The characteristics specify how syntactically interdependent the two units of an apposition are and their degree of semantic similarity. Each apposition in Figure 5.7 is assigned a number indicating the semantic category to which the apposition belongs and the number of syntactic criteria the apposition does not satisfy. These numbers are totalled to indicate precisely how appositional a particular construction is. The lower the number, the more centrally appositional the construction is.

Example 18a contains a construction that is a central apposition. The units of this apposition are coreferential and therefore semantically identical. In addition, the units are syntactically interdependent, satisfying all of the syntactic criteria for apposition: each unit in the apposition can be dropped (examples 18b and c), and the units can be interchanged (example 18d).

> (18a) *Mr Radkewicz, our director*, was in a hurry to move on. (SEU w.16.7.31–2)
> (18b) Our director was in a hurry to move on.
> (18c) Mr Radkewicz was in a hurry to move on.
> (18d) Our director, Mr Radkewicz, was in a hurry to move on.

Examples 19a and 20a, on the other hand, are not as appositional as the construction in example 18a. The units in each of these appositions are not coreferential. Instead, the first unit in each apposition refers cataphorically to the second unit, making the units semantically semi-identical rather than identical. In addition, the units satisfy only some of the syntactic criteria for apposition. While both units can be deleted in the first apposition (examples 19b and c), only the second unit can be deleted in the second apposition (example 20c), since the deletion of the first unit results in an unacceptable structure: a *to*-clause following a preposition (example 20b). In addition, marginal constructions result if the units of both appositions are interchanged (examples 19d and 20d).

> (19a) One aspect which concerns the Falklanders is *Lord Chalfont's – and the British Government's – assumption that they suffer great inconvenience through Argentina's cold-shouldering of them*. (SEU w.12.4.31)
> (19b) One aspect which concerns the Falklanders is that they suffer great inconvenience through Argentina's cold-shouldering of them.
> (19c) One aspect which concerns the Falklanders is Lord Chalfont's – and the British Government's – assumption.
> (19d) ?One aspect which concerns the Falklanders is that they suffer great inconvenience through Argentina's cold-shoulder-

Fig. 5.7 The gradient of central apposition to peripheral apposition

Example	Semantic category	No. of syntactic criteria not satisfied	Total
The leader of the group, John Smith, resigned	1	0	1
The writer Martin Amis is becoming famous	1	$\frac{1}{2}$	$1\frac{1}{2}$
The word ain't is common in colloquial English	1	1	2
The belief that teachers are underpaid is widespread	2	1	3
The worker's request to leave early was denied	2	2	4
Firefighter Sue Andrews was injured	3	$1\frac{1}{2}$	$4\frac{1}{2}$
Ed Jones, former mayor of Austin, plans to re-enter politics	3	2	5
A person like *Fran* should not exercise too vigorously	3	3	6

An apposition is given a figure of $\frac{1}{2}$ if it questionably satisfies a syntactic criterion

Semantic categories
1 The units are semantically identical
2 The units are semantically semi-identical
3 One unit is semantically included in the other unit

Syntactic criteria
1 The first unit can be deleted
2 The second unit can be deleted
3 The units can be interchanged

ing of them, Lord Chalfont's – and the British Government's – assumption.

(20a) He [Amos C. Barstow] spoke of *his desire to promote the abolition of slavery by peaceable means* and he compared John

Table 5.1. *Frequency of occurrence of various grammatical relations*

Relation	Occurrences per 1,000 words
Peripheral elements (e.g. adverbials)	8.1
Apposition	7.9
Modification	7.0
Complementation	4.4
Coordination	4.0

> Brown of Harper's Ferry to the John Brown of Rhode Island's colonial period. (Brown J58 1440–60)
> (20b) *He spoke of to promote the abolition of slavery by peaceable means.
> (20c) He spoke of his desire.
> (20d) *He spoke of to promote the abolition of slavery by peaceable means, his desire.

Example 21a contains a construction that is a peripheral apposition. Because the reference of the second unit is included in the reference of the first unit, the units are not semantically identical. In addition, the construction satisfies none of the syntactic criteria for apposition. Neither unit can be deleted (examples 21b and c), and the units cannot be interchanged (example 21d).

> (21a) If she had *something* like *knitting* that kept her happy all day, surely that was better than sitting. (LLC s.1.12 1064–8)
> (21b) *If she had like knitting that kept her happy all day...
> (21c) *If she had something like that kept her happy all day...
> (21d) *If she had knitting like something that kept her busy all day...

5.4 The relative frequency of apposition in relation to other grammatical relations

Biber (1988:75–8) calculates the frequency with which a number of grammatical constructions occurred in the London–Lund Corpus of spoken British English and the London–Oslo–Bergen Corpus of edited written British English. Table 5.1 matches these constructions with the grammatical relations that they realized and compares the frequency of these relations with the frequency of the relation of apposition in this study. As Table 5.1 demonstrates, apposition is a very frequently occurring grammatical relation. In the corpora investigated in this study, 7.9 appositions per thousand words occurred. In Biber's corpus, while constructions realizing the relation of peripheral elements occurred slightly more frequently than those realizing the relation of apposition, the other relations – modification, complementation, and coordination – occurred less frequently. The relatively frequent occurrence of the relation of apposition demonstrates that apposition is indeed an important grammatical relation in English.

5.5 Future research

Past studies of apposition have been marked by many disagreements and inconsistencies (1.1). To provide a clearer understanding of apposition, this study used three computer corpora of English to demonstrate that apposition is best understood as a grammatical relation having realizations with specific syntactic, semantic, and pragmatic characteristics.

Although much has been written about the other grammatical relations in English, relatively little of this research has investigated the occurrence of these relations in computer corpora.[2] For example, while numerous studies discuss the syntactic and semantic characteristics of coordinated constructions in English (cf., for instance, Quirk et al. 1985:918ff), no corpus study of coordination has yet been conducted. Such a study would reveal whether current linguistic descriptions of coordination adequately explain actual instances of coordination in corpora, whether the various types of coordination occur with equal or unequal frequency, and whether coordination usage varies by genre. Studies with similar foci should be conducted of the other grammatical relations. Results of such research will be of tremendous value: not only will they provide us with better descriptions of the various grammatical relations in English but they will give us information about their usage as well.

Appendix 1   Grammatical tags

(A) Corpus

1. Brown
2. LLC
3. SEU

(B) Genre

1. Press
2. Learned (scientific)
3. Learned (humanistic)
4. Fiction
5. Conversation: disparates
6. Conversation: equals
7. Conversation: intimates/equals
8. Conversation: intimates

(C) Sample

BROWN CORPUS

1–17	(A) = Press reportage
18–20	(B) = Press editorials
21–30	(J) = Learned writing (scientific)
31–40	(J) = Learned writing (humanistic)
41–4	(K) = General fiction
45–7	(L) = Mystery and detective fiction
48–52	(N) = Adventure and Western fiction
53–7	(P) = Romance and love story
58–60	(R) = Humorous fiction

1. A01	2. A02	3. A03	4. A04
5. A05	6. A06	7. A07	8. A08
9. A10	10. A11	11. A12	12. A16
13. A17	14. A19	15. A20	16. A21
17. A22	18. B08	19. B09	20. B11
21. J01	22. J02	23. J03	24. J04
25. J06	26. J09	27. J17	28. J24
29. J28	30. J33	31. J52	32. J53
33. J54	34. J57	35. J58	36. J59
37. J61	38. J63	39. J66	40. J67

41. K05	42. K16	43. K35	44. K29
45. L06	46. L19	47. L22	48. N02
49. N05	50. N08	51. N13	52. N25
53. P05	54. P09	55. P17	56. P22
57. P28	58. R01	59. R02	60. R03

LONDON–LUND CORPUS

61–6 = Disparates
67–72 = Equals
73–8 = Intimates/equals
79–84 = Intimates

61. S.3.5	62. S.3.3	63. S.3.4	64. S.3.2
65. S.3.1	66. S.3.6	67. S.1.13	68. S.1.12
69. S.2.2	70. S.2.3	71. S.2.9	72. S.2.10
73. S.2.11	74. S.2.6	75. S.1.6	76. S.1.11
77. S.1.9	78. S.1.10	79. S.1.4	80. S.2.8
81. S.1.2	82. S.1.3	83. S.1.8	84. S.1.7

SURVEY OF ENGLISH USAGE CORPUS

85–8 (w.9) = Learned writing (scientific)
89–92 (w.9) = Learned writing (humanistic)
93–100 (w.16) = Fiction
101–8 (w.12) = Press

85. w.9.6	86. w.9.7	87. w.9.8	88. w.9.9
89. w.9.1	90. w.9.2	91. w.9.3	92. w.9.4
93. w.16.1	94. w.16.2	95. w.16.3	96. w.16.4
97. w.16.5	98. w.16.6	99. w.16.7	100. w.16.8
101. w.12.1	102. w.12.2	103. w.12.3	104. w.12.4
105. w.12.5	106. w.12.6	107. w.12.7	108. w.12.8

(D) Reference

1. Generic
2. Specific
3. Not relevant

(E) Syntactic form

1. NP (−det) + proper NP
2. NP (d) + proper NP
3. Proper NP + NP (−det)
4. Proper NP + NP (d)
5. Proper NP + NP (i/a)
6. NP (i) + proper NP
7. Other appo proper NP
8. NP (i) + NP (i)
9. NP (d) + NP (d)
10. NP (i) + NP (d)

−det = Noun phrase lacking determiner
d = Definite noun phrase
i = Indefinite noun phrase
i/a = Indefinite attributive noun phrase

Pro = Pronoun
ing = -ing participle clause
abs = Absolute clause

11. NP (d)+NP (i)
13. Other appo common NP
15. NP with cardinal no.
17. Symbols, abbreviations
19. Pro (i)+NP (i)
21. Pro (i)+pro (i)
23. Other appo pro
25. NP (i)+*that*-clause
27. NP (i)+*to*-clause
29. Pro (d)+clause
31. NP (d)+sentence
33. Card number NP+sent
35. Other NP+sent
37. *Like*
39. NP (d)+*of*+ing
41. *Including*
43. *Particularly*
45. *For instance*
47. *Even*
49. *Specifically*
51. Proper NP+*or*+NP (i)
53. NP (d)+*or*+NP (d)
55. Other *or*
57. Adj phrase
59. Adv phrase
61. *to* infinitive
63. *that* clause
65. Dec sent
67. Exclamatory sent
69. Adj+NP
71. Adv+prep phrase
73. Non-nominal clauses
75. NP (d)+*of*+subordinate clause
77. NP (i)+other clause

12. NP (d)+NP (i/a)
14. Citations
16. Numbers (e.g. percentages)
18. Pro (d)+NP (d)
20. Pro (d)+NP (i/a)
22. NP (i)+pro (i)
24. NP (d)+*that*-clause
26. NP (d)+*to*-clause
28. NP (d)+other clause
30. NP (i)+sentence
32. Sent+NP (i/a)
34. Pro (d)+sent
36. *Such as*
38. NP (d)+*of*+NP
40. NP (d)+*of*+abs
42. *Especially*
44. *In particular*
46. *Mostly*
48. *Among them*
50. *Chiefly*
52. NP (i)+*or*+NP (i)
54. Proper NP+*or*+proper NP
56. Prep phrase
58. Pred phrase
60. Verb phrase
62. Clause with subor
64. Other clause appo
66. Interrog sent
68. NP+adj
70. Other SC appo
72. Other adv appo
74. Other non-nominal appo
76. NP (i)+NP (i/a)
78. *e.g.*

(F) Syntactic function

1. Subject (non-existential)
2. Subject (existential)
3. Direct object
4. Indirect object
5. Object of preposition
6. Subject complement
7. Object complement
8. Adverbial
9. Verb
10. No function

(G) Multiple apposition

1. Single apposition
2. Double apposition
3. Triple apposition

(H)   Juxtaposed/unjuxtaposed apposition

1. Juxtaposed
2. End-focus/weight
3. Syntactic constraints
4. Pronoun stress
5. Pragmatic expressions

(I)   Binary/non-binary apposition

1. Binary
2. Non-binary
3. Distinction not relevant

(J)   Optional markers of apposition

1. *That is*
2. *That is to say*
3. *Namely*
4. *In other words*
5. *Other*
6. No marker
7. *i.e.*
8. *e.g.*
9. *say*
10. *viz.*

(K)   Semantic relations

1. Strict coreference
2. Speaker coreference
3. Part/whole reference
4. Cataphoric reference
5. Absolute
6. Speaker
7. Clausal/sentential
8. Attribution
9. Non-syntagmatic hyponymy
10. Syntagmatic hyponymy

(L)   Semantic classes

1. Characterization
2. Appellation
3. Identification
4. Exemplification
5. Particularization
6. Self-correction
7. Paraphrase
8. Reorientation

(M)   Restrictive/nonrestrictive apposition

1. Restrictive
2. Nonrestrictive
3. Not relevant

Appendix 2   Appositions in individual samples of the corpora

Genre/sample	No. of appositions	Appositions per 1,000 words
FICTION (BROWN)		
K05	8	3.0
K16	13	16.5
K25	21	10.5
K29	7	3.5
L06	7	3.5
L19	6	3.0
L22	21	10.5
N02	11	5.5
N05	13	6.5
N08	14	7.0
N13	3	1.5
N25	4	2.0
P05	9	4.5
P09	23	11.5
P17	16	8.0
P22	15	7.5
P28	9	4.5
R01	8	4.0
R02	20	10.0
R03	16	8.0
FICTION (SEU)		
W.16.1	29	5.8
W.16.2	20	4.0
W.16.3	21	4.2
W.16.4	20	4.0
W.16.5	40	8.0
W.16.6	13	2.6

Appendix 2 (*cont.*)

Genre/sample	No. of appositions	Appositions per 1,000 words
w.16.7	23	4.6
w.16.8	35	7.0
CONVERSATION (INTIMATES)		
S.1.2	26	5.2
S.1.3	40	8.0
S.1.4	18	3.6
S.1.7	28	5.6
S.1.8	22	4.4
S.2.8	24	4.8
CONVERSATION (EQUALS)		
S.1.12	19	3.8
S.1.13	27	5.4
S.2.2	26	5.2
S.2.3	36	7.2
S.2.9	32	6.4
S.2.10	29	5.8
CONVERSATION (DISPARATES)		
S.3.1	26	5.2
S.3.2	35	7.0
S.3.3	27	5.4
S.3.4	39	7.8
S.3.5	47	9.4
S.3.6	49	9.8
CONVERSATION (INTIMATES/EQUALS)		
S.1.6	54	10.8
S.1.9	35	7.0
S.1.10	26	5.2
S.1.11	22	4.4
S.2.6	44	8.8
S.2.11	47	9.4
SCIENTIFIC (BROWN)		
J01	2	1.0
J02	12	6.0
J03	7	3.5
J04	5	2.5
J06	7	3.5
J09	11	5.5
J17	15	7.5
J24	18	9.0

Appendix 2 (*cont.*)

Genre/sample	No. of appositions	Appositions per 1,000 words
J28	30	15.0
J33	25	12.5
HUMANISTIC (BROWN)		
J52	22	11.0
J53	22	11.0
J54	4	2.0
J57	22	11.0
J58	14	7.0
J59	12	6.0
J61	14	7.0
J63	26	13.0
J66	37	18.5
J67	7	3.5
SCIENTIFIC (SEU)		
W.9.6	47	9.4
W.9.7	33	6.6
W.9.8	44	8.8
W.9.9	74	14.6
HUMANISTIC (SEU)		
W.9.1	107	21.4
W.9.2	42	8.4
W.9.3	29	5.8
W.9.4	67	13.4
PRESS (BROWN)		
A01	27	13.5
A02	20	10.0
A03	14	7.0
A04	15	8.5
A05	16	8.0
A06	19	9.5
A07	22	11.0
A08	18	9.0
A10	20	10.0
A11	34	17.0
A12	50	25.0
A16	46	23.0
A17	14	7.0
A19	20	10.0
A20	40	20.0

Appendix 2 (*cont.*)

Genre/sample	No. of appositions	Appositions per 1,000 words
A21	27	13.5
A22	20	10.0
B08	26	13.0
B09	7	3.5
B11	15	7.5
Press (SEU)		
W.12.1	65	13.0
W.12.2	81	16.2
W.12.3	45	9.0
W.12.4	40	8.0
W.12.5	32	6.4
W.12.6	42	8.4
W.12.7	50	10.0
W.12.8	39	7.8

Notes

1 Apposition as a grammatical relation

1 Unless otherwise noted, I have italicized the appositions in example sentences.
2 In the examples from Curme, only the second unit of an apposition is italicized because Curme considers only the second unit to be an apposition.
3 See 3.1 for a complete discussion of the semantic relations existing between units in apposition.
4 The grammatical relations listed in Fig. 1.1 are taken from Matthews (1981), which contains a detailed discussion of grammatical relations in English.
5 For more information on problem-oriented tagging programs, see de Haan (1984) and Tottie et al. (1984), which employed this kind of program to study, respectively, postmodifiers and synthetic and analytic negation.
6 See Mindt (1988) for more information on the use of SPSS to study corpus data.
7 Not all of the statistical information cited in this study was obtained from the tagging routine described in this section. Additional information was needed after the program was created and was obtained by manual analysis of certain sections of the corpora.

2 The syntax of apposition

1 This section contains both central and peripheral appositions. For a discussion of the syntactic and semantic gradients of apposition, see 2.5 and 3.4.
2 In examples taken from the London-Lund Corpus of Spoken British English, the prosodic transcription has been removed, and the examples rewritten in standard orthographic form.
3 Appositions like those in examples 5 and 6 are discussed in greater detail in 3.3, which deals with restrictive and nonrestrictive apposition, and in 4.4.2.3, which discusses stylistic and dialectal differences in the use of certain kinds of appositions.
  The status of the constructions in example 5 is somewhat controversial. While such constructions are considered appositions in this study and in Quirk et al. (1985:1319), in Bell (1988) they are termed "pseudo-titles" and in Rydén (1975) they are called "noun-name" collocations. See 2.5.4.1 for a more detailed discussion of the gradient that these appositions are on.

4 Definite noun phrases contain a definite article (e.g. *the child*), a possessive noun (e.g. *Jane's addiction*), or a possessive pronoun (e.g. *our child*).

5 The terms "attributive indefinite" article and "specific indefinite" article are taken from Burton-Roberts (1976). Although these terms make a semantic rather than a syntactic distinction between noun phrases, the distinction becomes relevant in 3.1, which contains a discussion of the semantic relations that exist between certain kinds of noun phrases. Hereafter, noun phrases containing an attributive indefinite article will simply be called "attributive noun phrases" and those containing specific indefinite noun phrases "indefinite noun phrases."

6 See 2.3 for a more detailed discussion of unjuxtaposed appositions such as the one in example 40. Although constructions of this type are typically termed "right dislocations" (Quirk *et al.* 1985:310), they are appositional in many respects. The units in such constructions are coreferential, a semantic relation that many units in apposition have (3.1.1.1). In addition, if the pronoun in the first unit and the noun phrase in the second unit are juxtaposed, a marker of apposition can be inserted between the units:

Strange, it was *she*, [i.e.] *Dinah*, who had dreamed always of living in the country, of running a small farm. (SEU w.16.1.17–3)

7 See 3.1.1.2 for a more detailed discussion of the semantic structure of constructions containing these kinds of obligatory markers of apposition. Also, not all of the obligatory markers discussed in this section exclusively join units in apposition. A marker such as *particularly* can simply be used to focus a constituent: *John was particularly upset with his performance on the exam.*

8 For exceptions, see Table 2.17.

9 Although not found in most scholarly grammars, the term predicate phrase (which originated in Chomsky 1965) is useful for distinguishing a constituent that is larger than a verb phrase but smaller than a clause.

10 The exceptions, of course, are sentences in apposition (2.1.4.2), which have no syntactic function. See 2.2 for a more detailed discussion of the syntactic function of units in apposition.

11 In some appositions, it was possible to determine a syntactic function for only the first unit in the apposition. In the example below, only the first unit (*three questions*) has a syntactic function; the second unit (the three interrogative sentences ending the example) has no function.

The force of the author's analysis (if indeed it has any force) can be felt by the reader, I believe, only after *three questions* have been successfully answered. (1) *What allows us to think that the patient had no third-dimensional representations when his eyes were closed?* (2) *What evidence is there that he was psychically blind?* (3) *How can we be sure that his sense of touch was not profoundly disturbed by his head injury?* (Brown J53 320–70)

In other appositions, it was not possible to determine a syntactic function for either unit. In the example below, because two sentences are in apposition, it is not possible to determine a syntactic function for either unit:

He found himself going through the weeks like an automaton. [That is to say] He taught and corrected and lectured; and in the evenings did the same. (SEU w.16.7.37–3)

12 In his study of postmodification of noun phrases, de Haan (1989:117) found that no indirect objects in his corpus contained any postmodification. He argues

that this situation existed because indirect objects have prepositional phrase paraphrases, paraphrases that move the indirect object into a position promoting end-weight: object of the preposition *to* or *for*. As a result of this process, the very awkward example a below, as de Haan observes, becomes the much more acceptable example b.

(a) *?I have given *the man that you pointed out to me* the papers.
(b) I have given the papers to *the man that you pointed out to me*. [italics in original]

13 An invented example is cited here because no fully appositional construction of this form occurred in any of the corpora. See 3.3.1 for a discussion of the rarity of this kind of restrictive apposition.

3 The semantics of apposition

1 Not all nominal appositions contained units that were coreferential noun phrases. Some consisted of units between which the relation of attribution existed. See 3.1.2.2 for a discussion of the difference between units that were coreferential and units related by the relation of attribution.

2 The potential referents of noun phrases in English is quite extensive and quite complicated. See Webber (1979:1/15–1/19) for a discussion of the range of referents that noun phrases in English can have.

3 Like many semanticists, Cornish does not distinguish between anaphora and cataphora, viewing cataphora as simply a type of anaphora.

4 Unlike Cornish, many semanticists do not make a clear distinction between coreference and anaphora, often using the terms interchangeably. As a result, many semanticists would allow for coreference of noun phrases and clauses and sentences. Hirst (1981:4), for instance, maintains that all instances of anaphora involve coreference, and in a later section on types of anaphoric constructions discusses "prosentential reference" (pp. 13–14), reference between a pronoun and an entire predication, as in the example he cites below:

The president was shot while riding in a motorcade down a major Dallas boulevard today; *it* caused a panic on Wall Street. [italics in original]

5 Hyponymous appositions are not to be confused with appositions whose units are in a part/whole relation to one another (3.1.1.3), even though in both relations there is a subordinate/superordinate relationship between the units. The main difference between the two relations is that in a part/whole relation there is "referential" inclusion between the units, whereas in a relation of hyponymy, there is "meaning" inclusion between the units. In example 48, the meaning of the second unit is included within the meaning of the first unit. In the example below, on the other hand, the reference of the second unit, *the Prometheus*, is included within the reference of the first unit, *an early play*.

Do you think I should take *an early play*, like *the Prometheus*? (LLC s.1.4 1204–5)

See Lyons (1977:311) and Leech (1981:93) for a more detailed discussion of the difference between meaning inclusion and referential inclusion.

6 Quirk *et al* (1985:1311) list a variety of expressions that can be used to mark a synonymous relationship between units in apposition: *(more) simply, in*

scientific terminology, technically (speaking), and so forth. However, none of these expressions occurred in any of the appositions of this type in the corpora; only the markers *that is (to say)*, *in other words*, and *or* were found.

4   The pragmatics of apposition

1 Following Firbas (1986:44), I am defining old information as information that is "retrievable from the immediate context..." and new information as information that is "irretrievable" from the immediate context. If this definition of new and old information is not used, certain kinds of constructions do not qualify pragmatically as appositions because they appear to contain only old information. For instance, in the example below, the second unit of the apposition appears to contain old information (*Herman*) because it repeats information introduced earlier into the discourse.

> Herman we ought to say a word about before we keep him on the list...I think Jack advised him that he couldn't maintain his application here having more or less promised to go to Malta...*He*'s a very interesting candidate, *Herman*, I think, although he's becoming too old, too. (LLC s.2.6 724–59)

However, according to Firbas, the last instance of *Herman* would be new (i.e. "unknown") information rather than old information: the first instance of *Herman* occurs so far back in the discourse (33 tone units) that by the time it is reintroduced it is no longer retrievable but irretrievable and therefore new rather than old information.

2 See 2.1.3 for a discussion of obligatory markers of apposition, markers that for syntactic and semantic reasons must be used to introduce the second unit of an apposition.

3 Because the genres of the corpora were of unequal length, it would have been misleading to use only frequency counts to compare the number of appositions occurring in the various genres. Consequently, a formula from Biber (1988:76) was used to calculate the number of appositions per thousand words, a formula allowing for valid comparisons of texts of unequal length.

4 Appositions within the class of reorientation consist of coreferential noun phrases of equal specificity (3.2.3.2). In this kind of apposition, the second unit refocuses the reference of the first unit. Appositions within the semantic classes of exemplification and particularization consist of units which are either hyponyms or in a part/whole relation to one another (3.2.1.3 and 3.2.1.4). In appositions within the class of exemplification, the second unit provides an example of the very general first unit; in appositions within the class of particularization, the second unit focuses either the meaning or the reference of the first unit.

5 Appositions serving a corrective function are different from those serving a clarifying function. In an apposition whose second unit corrects the first unit, the first unit contains an error that the second unit corrects. On the other hand, in an apposition whose second unit clarifies the reference or meaning of the first unit, the first unit is not an error but rather a word or phrase requiring some kind of clarification.

6 Appositions within the class of paraphrase also contain repetition: the second unit "repeats" the meaning of the first. Repetition is important in conversation

(4.1.2). Consequently, this is another communicative function that this kind of apposition serves in speech.

7 See 2.5 for a more detailed discussion of the syntactic interrelationships between various types of apposition.

8 There are other examples in journalistic writing of the importance of concision in press reportage. For instance, in a study of punctuation practice in the Brown Corpus (Meyer 1987b), it was found that coordinated constructions were more lightly punctuated in journalistic writing than in learned writing. In a compound series, the serial comma was usually omitted in journalistic writing (example a below) but retained in the learned writing (Meyer 1987b:102):

(a) The fire ant is thought to infest approximately two million acres of land in Georgia, attacking *crops, young wildlife and livestock* and can be a serious health menace to humans who are allergic to its venom, Blasingame said. (Brown A22 1730–60)

In compound sentences, it was quite common in journalistic writing for the clauses to be either unpunctuated or lightly punctuated with a comma (Meyer 1987b:54):

(b) The Rev. Richard Freeman of Texas City officiated and Charles Pabor and Mrs. Marvin Hand presented music. (Brown A17 1550–80)

In learned writing, in contrast, such constructions were more heavily punctuated, either with commas or with semicolons.

5 Apposition in the grammar of English

1 Because bar graphs are used to indicate frequencies in this section, the various genres of spoken English were left out of the analysis, since unequal proportions of spoken English were sampled: 30,000 words from each genre as opposed to 80,000 words from the genres of press, learned writing, and fiction.

2 Some notable exceptions include Greenbaum's (1969) study of adverbials (a type of peripheral element), de Haan's (1989) study of postmodification, and Mair's (1990) study of complementation.

References

Aarts, F. 1971. On the distribution of noun-phrase types in English clause structure. *Lingua* 26: 252–64.

Aarts, J. and Meijs, W. (eds.) 1984. *Corpus linguistics*. Amsterdam: Rodopi.

Akmajian, A., Demers, R. A. and Harnish, R. M. 1984. *Linguistics: an introduction to language and communication*. 2nd edn. Cambridge, MA: MIT Press.

Allerton, D. J. 1979. *Essentials of grammatical theory*. London: Routledge & Kegan Paul.

de Beaugrande, R. and Dressler, W. 1981. *Introduction to text linguistics*. London: Longman.

Bell, A. 1988. The British base and the American connection in New Zealand media English. *American Speech* 63: 326–44.

Biber, D. 1988. *Variation across speech and writing*. Cambridge: CUP.

Bloomfield, L. 1933. *Language*. New York: Rinehart & Winston.

Burton-Roberts, N. 1975. Nominal apposition. *Foundations of Language* 13: 391–419.

1976. On the generic indefinite article. *Language* 52: 427–48.

Chomsky, N. 1965. *Aspects of the theory of syntax*. Cambridge, MA: MIT Press.

Copperud, R. 1964. *A dictionary of usage and style*. New York: Hawthorn Books.

Cornish, F. 1986. *Anaphoric relations in English and French*. London: Routledge.

Cruse, D. A. 1986. *Lexical semantics*. Cambridge: CUP.

Curme, G. 1931. *Syntax*. Boston: D. C. Heath & Co.

Donnellan, K. S. 1979. Speaker reference, descriptions, and anaphora. In P. A. French, T. E. Uehling and H. K. Wettstein (eds.) *Contemporary perspectives in the philosophy of language*. Minneapolis: University of Minnesota Press. 28–44.

Erman, B. 1986. Some pragmatic expressions in English conversation. In G. Tottie and I. Backlund (eds.) *English in speech and writing*. Stockholm: Almqvist & Wiksell. 131–47.

Firbas, J. 1980. Post-intonation-centre prosodic shade in the modern English clause. In S. Greenbaum, G. Leech and J. Svartvik (eds.) *Studies in English linguistics for Randolph Quirk*. London: Longman. 125–33.

1986. On the dynamics of written communication in the light of the theory of functional sentence perspective. In S. Greenbaum and C. Cooper (eds.) *Studying writing*. Beverly Hills, CA: Sage. 40–71.

Francis, W. N. 1958. *The structure of American English*. New York: Ronald.

Fries, C. C. 1952. *The structure of English*. New York: Harcourt.

Garnham, A. R. *et al.* 1982. Slips of the tongue in the London-Lund Corpus of Spontaneous Conversation. In A. Cutler (ed.) *Slips of the tongue and language production.* New York: Mouton. 251–63.

Greenbaum, S. 1969. *Studies in English adverbial usage.* London: Longman.

1985. 25th anniversary of the Survey of English Usage. *World Englishes* 4: 261–5.

Greenbaum, S. and Whitcut, J. 1988. *Longman guide to English usage.* London: Longman.

de Haan, P. 1984. Problem-oriented tagging of English Corpus data. In Aarts and Meijs (1984). 123–39.

1987. Exploring the linguistic database: noun phrase complexity and language variation. In Meijs, W. (ed.), *Corpus linguistics and beyond.* Amsterdam: Rodopi. 151–65.

1989. *Postmodifying clauses in the English noun phrase.* Amsterdam: Rodopi.

Halliday, M. and Hasan, R. 1976. *Cohesion in English.* London: Longman.

Haugen, E. 1953. On resolving the close apposition. *American Speech* 28: 165–70.

Hirst, G. 1981. *Anaphora in natural language understanding.* Berlin: Springer.

Hockett, C. 1955. Attribution and apposition. *American Speech* 30: 99–102.

Huddleston, R. 1984. *Introduction to the grammar of English.* Cambridge: CUP.

The Independent style book, 2nd edn. 1988. London: *The Independent.*

Jespersen, O. 1961. *A modern English grammar on historical principles.* London: Allen & Unwin.

Johansson, S. and Hofland, K. 1989. *Frequency analysis of English vocabulary and grammar.* Oxford: Clarendon Press.

Kučera, H. and Francis, W. N. 1967. *Computational analysis of present-day American English.* Providence: Department of Linguistics, Brown University.

Leech, G. 1981. *Semantics,* 2nd edn. New York: Penguin.

Lucas, M. 1974. The surface structure of relative clauses. *Linguistics* 139: 83–120.

Lyons, J. 1977. *Semantics,* vols. 1 and 2. Cambridge: CUP

Mair, C. 1990. *Infinitival complement clauses in English.* Cambridge: CUP.

Matthews, P. H. 1981. *Syntax.* Cambridge: CUP.

Meyer, C. 1987a. Apposition in English. *Journal of English Linguistics* 20(1): 101–21.

1987b. *A linguistic study of American punctuation.* New York: Peter Lang.

1989. Restrictive apposition: an indeterminate category. *English Studies* 70: 147–66.

Mindt, D. (ed.) 1988. *EDV in der Angewandten Linguistik. Ziele–Methoden–Ergebnisse. [The computer in applied linguistics. aims–methods–results]* Frankfurt-am-Main: Diesterweg.

Nie, N. *et al.* 1975. *Statistical package for the social sciences,* 2nd edn. New York: McGraw-Hill.

Norwood, J. 1954. The loose appositive in present-day English. *American Speech* 29: 267–71.

The Oxford Guide to the English Language. 1984. Oxford: OUP.

Quirk, R., Greenbaum, S., Leech, G. and Svartvik, J. 1985. *A comprehensive grammar of the English language.* London: Longman.

Rydén, Mats. 1975. Noun-name collocations in British English newspaper language. *Studia Neophilologica* 67: 14–39.

Sopher, H. 1971. Apposition. *English Studies* 52: 401–12.

Svartvik, J. (ed.) 1990. *The London-Lund Corpus of Spoken English: description and research*. Lund Studies in English 82. Lund: Lund University Press.

Svartvik, J. and Quirk, R. (eds.) 1980. *A corpus of English conversation*. Lund Studies in English 56. Lund: Lund University Press.

Taglicht, J. 1977. Relative clauses as postmodifiers: meaning, syntax and intonation. In W. Bald and R. Ilson (eds.) *Studies in English usage: the resources of a present-day corpus for linguistic analysis*. Frankfurt: Peter Lang. 73–108.

Tannen, D. 1987. Repetition and variation as spontaneous formulaicity in conversation. *Language* 63: 574–605.

Tottie, G. *et al.* 1984. Tagging negative sentences in LOB and LLC. In Aarts and Meijs (1984). 173–84.

Webber, B. 1979. *A formal approach to discourse anaphora*. New York: Garland.

Williams, J. 1979. Defining complexity. *College English* 40: 595–609.

    1981. *Style*. Glenview, IL: Scott, Foresman.

Ziff, P. 1960. *Semantic analysis*. Ithaca, NY: Cornell University Press.

Index

For EU product safety concerns, contact us at Calle de José Abascal, 56–1°,
28003 Madrid, Spain or eugpsr@cambridge.org.